Surveying Fiberglass Sailboats

A Step-by-Step Guide for Buyers and Owners

Henry C. Mustin

International Marine
Camden, Maine

To Sarah

Published by International Marine

10 9 8 7 6 5 4 3 2 1

Copyright © 1994 International Marine, an imprint of TAB Books. TAB Books is a division of McGraw-Hill, Inc.

Library of Congress Cataloging-in-Publication Data
Mustin, Henry.
    Surveying fiberglass sailboats : a step-by-step guide for buyers and owners /
Henry Mustin.
        p.   cm.
    Includes index.
    ISBN 0-87742-347-4
    1. Fiberglass boats--Inspection. I. Title.
VM321.M87 1994
623.8'207--dc20   93-40779
                                                          CIP

Questions regarding the content of this book should be addressed to:
International Marine
P.O. Box 220
Camden, ME 04843

Questions regarding the ordering of this book should be addressed to:
TAB Books
A Division of McGraw-Hill, Inc.
Blue Ridge Summit, PA 17294
1-800-233-1128

Surveying Fiberglass Sailboats is printed on acid-free paper.

Unless otherwise noted, illustrations are by Benjamin D. Shreve.
Unless otherwise noted, photographs are by Sam Murfitt.
Printed by Fairfield Arcata, Fairfield, PA
Design by Faith Hague
Production by Molly Mulhern
Edited by Jonathan Eaton and Dennis Caprio

Contents

Introduction

The craft of surveying fiberglass boats is relatively new. Its origins coincide with the early construction of fiberglass boats, beginning in the late 1950s with the introduction of the 28-foot Pearson Triton sloop. Prior to that time, marine surveyors comprised a small group of classification surveyors—representing the Salvage Association (Lloyds), Bureau Veritas, and others—or insurance surveyors. The small number of independent surveyors worked primarily with small craft of wood or steel.

The need for more small-craft surveyors rose with the number of boats built in the 1960s and 1970s, and for the most part this need was filled by experienced individuals whose training and background were firmly rooted in wooden boats. Therefore, many of the techniques used in surveying fiberglass boats were taken from those used in evaluating a wooden hull. The most common of these techniques is the percussion test—tapping the hull with a hammer. A lot of the terminology, too, is the same. For instance, the term *scantling*, which refers to the size of a frame or other wood member, is still used to denote the thickness of a fiberglass hull. The terms *longitudinal, floor, bulkhead,* and *stem* also have made the transition to fiberglass construction.

Surveyors still look for *fairness* (smoothness) in the hull's surface, and still inspect the attachment of the keel ballast, the mechanical fastening of the deck to the hull, chainplate installations, and the like. The one technique that did not immediately carry over to surveying fiberglass is the probe. The thickness of a wood boat's planking is a given, and by using a probe (ice pick or sharp blade), the surveyor can ascertain how much good wood remains in any plank, frame, or longitudinal stiffener. He cannot do the same with a fiberglass hull, and nearly 25 years passed before the use of ultrasonics allowed surveyors to calculate with any accuracy the thickness of a fiberglass hull.

To my knowledge, the first fiberglass-specific testing tool that surveyors used was the Barcol hardness tester. It is a manually controlled instrument that measures the *cure*, or hardness, of fiberglass laminates by means of a needle-type probe inserted into the finished laminate. If the resins have failed to *set up* properly ("kick"), the probe encounters little resistance; if the resins have set up, the resistance is greater. Calibration allows the surveyor to determine whether the laminate has cured satisfactorily or not. This tool, though widely used in the 1960s and 1970s, has lost its appeal and is rarely used now except by builders. It should be used a great deal more, in my opinion, especially when blistering is present.

The next technological leap in the evaluation of fiberglass hulls came with the introduction of the moisture meter (such as the Sovereign Moisture Meter), a tool long used in the timber trades for monitoring the drying process of wood. The instrument transmits microwaves through a scanning head, then relays the feedback signals to a calibrated dial, which allows the surveyor to evaluate the moisture content of a given area of a hull. Surveyors in the U.S. did not use this tool until the early 1980s, and it changed the face of surveying forever. We had assumed that fiberglass hulls would last indefinitely, and we felt that fiberglass laminates were more or less waterproof. Both surmises proved wrong. Suddenly, boats were failing surveys in record numbers due to high moisture content in the hull and deck laminates, in many cases causing osmotic blisters. As we had nothing else to evaluate the likelihood of blisters appearing on a hull in the future, the moisture meter was and is considered the best tool for the purpose. On the other hand, it is also one of the most misused instruments ever to come down the pike. I know many surveyors who use the moisture meter on an absolute basis, even though the manufacturer specifically warns against this and recommends using the relative scale. Its great use is to locate very high concentrations of moisture, such as around a stanchion or seacock, relative to readings taken from the rest of the hull. But it has limitations. There are numerous models on the market, and some will not read through surface coatings (paint), while others supposedly will. Some read the gelcoat only, while others read the inner layers of the laminate. If the instrument in use is calibrated to read surface moisture, one is prevented from making definitive conclusions about subsurface moisture, and vice versa.

In the 1980s, small and portable ultrasonic gauges became available at a high price (about $2,000). Mainly used without oscilloscopes, these instruments, which send a sonar signal and measure the return time, allow a surveyor to accurately measure the consistency of the skin thickness and the thickening of the laminate (when the hull is so constructed) below the waterline and near the centerline. Its high price has kept this instrument from wide use in fiberglass hull surveying today.

By my calculations, approximately 6,000 independent surveyors currently work in the United States alone. This number is quite a leap from the 20 or so that in 1960 formed the National Association of Marine Surveyors (NAMS). This organization now numbers about 500 members and has since 1980 operated a certification program, through which successful candidates after passing a written examination are awarded the Certified Marine Surveyor (CMS) designation. Today's surveyors are better grounded in the methods and techniques of fiberglass construction than their wood-boat predecessors were, and they have the benefit of the technology discussed above to help them evaluate a vessel. The single biggest problem in surveying today is the absence of regulation, which makes selecting a surveyor increasingly difficult for boatowners or prospective owners.

My goals in writing this book are:

1. to help the buyers of new and used boats screen out the bad from the good;
2. to educate consumers in the craft and business of surveying so that they will be able to hire a good surveyor and get better value for the fee;
3. to enable the boatowner to inspect his own boat, identify incipient problems, and design a maintenance program;
4. to prepare the buyer or owner for the practicality and cost of repairs and improvements and their probable effect on the boat's market value;
5. to identify certain common flaws in the way boats were or are being built so that the reader can be on guard against these in new or old boats;
6. and to answer the question, "When is a boat too far gone to resuscitate?"

Chapter 1

The Raw Materials of a Fiberglass Boat

To understand what a surveyor looks for, you have to know how a boat goes together. This chapter examines the raw materials of fiberglass hulls and decks, starting with the fibers themselves, then the resins with which they're laid up, and then the various core materials and their applications. We'll postpone such vital aspects of construction as bulkheads, stiffeners, hull-to-deck joints, and ballast placement until later chapters, when we talk about how to evaluate their condition.

Fiberglass

Fiberglass is made by extruding molten glass through holes of various sizes to form filaments, also known as *spun glass*. These are then bundled together into strands, which are woven, knitted, or amassed into fabrics. When short pieces of strand are laid down in random orientation and compressed into a sheet held together with a resin-soluble binder, the result is *chopped-strand mat* or *CSM*. Mat is designated by its weight per square foot (usually ¾ to 3 ounces), and because of the great adhesive ability of its short strands, it is used to separate layers of other fabric types in the *lay-up*, or *laminate*, of a fiberglass hull or deck. The random orientation of its strands makes it highly water-resistant, which is one reason why mat is used for the outside layer of a hull, immediately under the gelcoat.

Woven roving is a coarse weave of thick, heavy strands. When used in a hull lay-up (as it commonly is), it builds up laminate thickness fast, and

Chopped-strand mat (2¼-ounce).

it has great tensile strength (more than twice that of mat) along its warp and weft strands, which are at 90 degrees to each other. Its strength is lower on the bias, or at 45 degrees to the warp and weft strands. Because resin does not adhere very uniformly to the coarse weave in a mold, layers of woven roving do not bond well with each other and so should be alternated with layers of mat to maintain high interlaminate shear

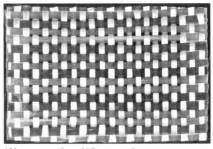

Woven roving (18-ounce).

strength; the majority of cruising fiberglass sailboat hulls have been built from alternating layers of woven roving and mat, with the roving usually weighing 18 or more ounces per square yard.

Fiberglass *cloth* is essentially a light woven roving (less than 10 ounces) with an open weave. It makes a strong, excellent laminating material, but it does not build thickness as fast as roving. Each layer of cloth in a laminate adds about .016 inch thickness, whereas a layer of 24-ounce roving adds about .035 inch. Cloth is a good material to use selectively in areas of the boat requiring extra strength—such as the stem, keel stubby, deck flanges, transom corners, and under deck hardware.

Strands must be coated, or sized, before they are woven so they do not fly apart in the loom; when the coating is later burned off, the strands lose some of their strength, and the crimps induced by weaving also cause loss of strength. In *unidirectional rovings* the strands are all parallel and are cross-stitched together with light fibers rather than woven. Thus, unidirectional rovings are stronger along the strands than woven rovings, though they have little strength at 90 degrees to the strand run. Unidirectionals (UDs) are well suited to use in frames, longitudinal stiffeners, or deck beams. Two layers of

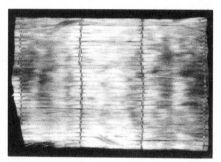

Unidirectional roving (13-ounce).

unidirectional with their strands oriented at 90 degrees can be stitched together to make a *biaxial roving*, which is stronger in both directions than a weave of the same weight, though harder to handle and to wet out with resin. When a third layer is added at yet another orientation, a *triaxial roving* results.

These finished products provide the strength of a hull or deck. When added to a resin matrix and properly cured, the result is fiberglass-reinforced plastic (FRP). Fiberglass strands are not water-resistant in themselves, and require a coating, or sizing, to protect them from deterioration. If the finished hull is to be resistant to osmotic blisters, the strands must be properly sized and wetted out with resins; otherwise, exposure to moisture—both fresh and salt water—may cause a chemical reaction. (As mentioned, strands are sized prior to weaving, but then, frequently, that sizing is removed and another sizing more compatible with the resin to be used is added.)

The principal fiber used in hull molding is E-glass, a low-alkaline glass that draws well and has stiffness, strength, and fairly good weathering properties. E-glass, however, loses about 50 percent of its strength when it is sized and woven. To avoid this loss of strength, other fibers can be used instead, but at a greater cost. The high-performance glass used in North America and the United Kingdom is S-glass (the French equivalent is called R-glass), the mechanical virtues of which can be 20 to 40 percent higher than those of E-glass. Furthermore, the better sizing protection possible with S-glass prevents loss of strength associated with attack by water, so a hull constructed with S-glass will be much less likely to develop osmotic blistering. S-glass is 5 to 10 times more expensive than E-glass, however, and is therefore seldom used in production boats.

Specialty Fibers

Two well-known fibers used effectively in one-off custom builds, limited-production yachts, and specialized applications are Kevlar and carbon fiber. Kevlar is an *aramid* (nylon) fiber, used in its Kevlar 49 designation. It has, in a strength-to-weight ratio, five times the strength of steel and twice the strength of S-glass. It also has a greater tensile modulus (resistance to failure from stretching) than S-glass, and it costs more. Low in compressive strength, Kevlar is best used in conjunction with E- and S-glasses to overcome this deficiency. It has been used, for example, to reinforce the topsides of racing boats.

Carbon fiber is a type of acrylic fiber, and variations of it depend to a large extent on the amount of carbon in the finished product. Because carbon fibers are processed at very high temperature (3,000 degrees F) and in limited volume, the cost is high (though it has been coming down in recent years), some 40 to 100 percent more than that of E-glass. The main advantage of carbon fiber is its stiffness, and it has found its principal application as a spar material (in boats built by Freedom Yachts, for example), since reduced weight aloft improves the stability of a sailboat. Because of its poor impact strength, it is seldom used in hulls.

Resins

We use the term *matrix* to denote "something within which something else originates or develops." Resins have little strength in themselves, but they provide the matrix within which the strength-giving fibers are shaped and bonded. Thus, we speak of FRP construction. The two types of applications we will discuss are gelcoat resins and laminating resins.

A successful fiberglass hull and deck need a compatible resin system. By compatible I mean that the gelcoat resins have to be compatible with the laminating resins, and the laminating resins should have the best qualities to blend with the reinforcing fibers so that these two elements work together, giving the greatest strength. Gelcoats in production builds are usually sprayed into female molds and form the exterior of the hull and deck shell. As such, the gelcoat has to be cosmetically pleasing, and also resistant to scratching and the damaging effects of ultraviolet light. In addition, the gelcoat must protect the inner laminates from moisture, retain its color well, and withstand impacts. *Polyester resins* appear to produce the best gelcoats, and they should be *isophthalic*, rather than *orthophthalic*, to improve their water-resistance. Since there is no reinforcement in the gelcoat, the mixture is thixotropic, which simply means it has been chemically "gelled up" so that it doesn't run when it's sprayed into the mold. Laminating resins do not have to be thixotropic because they are absorbed into the reinforcing fibers.

One of the reasons we had so many problems with osmotic blisters in the early 1980s was a gradual thinning of the gelcoat surfaces from those used in

7

boats constructed between 1958 and 1978. Consider that those early boats, literally thousands of them, used orthophthalic polyester resins, and very few ever blistered. Why? The gelcoats were applied, many by hand, to a thickness of between $\frac{1}{16}$ and $\frac{3}{32}$ inch. From the late 1970s into the early 1980s, when blisters began to proliferate in alarming numbers, builders gradually thinned out the gelcoats to $\frac{1}{32}$ inch. While gelcoat is not a perfect barrier against osmosis, it remains the best we have in conventional resins.

The choice of resins and reinforcements used in boatbuilding is heavily influenced by cost. We have the technology to build far better boats than we do, but we can't do it at a cost the average buyer can afford. So, boat manufacturers keep using the most cost-effective materials, sometimes adding better materials to overcome problems, such as hull blisters, but doing so in a hybrid manner. For example, polyester resins, being the least expensive, are still widely used for laminating, but some *vinylester* resins might be added in the bottom of a boat to make a more water-resistant laminate there. Vinylester resins handle in much the same way as polyesters, and in addition to being more water-resistant, they do not shrink quite as much when they cure, so less is required to maintain good interlaminate bonds. Although builders can construct better hulls from vinylester resins—and many do— these boats are more expensive than those built with polyester resins.

Epoxies are clearly the finest laminating resins we have. They shrink considerably less on curing than either of the ester group, they form a superior resin-to-fiber bond, they have excellent loading strength, and they are the most water-resistant. Epoxy resins are a "two-part" system requiring a *hardener*, which initiates a polymerization or cross-linking of the resin molecules.

The high cost of epoxy, some three times more than a polyester system, has made builders reluctant to use it, despite its superior performance. It is more difficult to work with as a laminating resin and can be quite toxic. Epoxy is not suitable for gelcoat because of its sensitivity to ultraviolet radiation.

All of these resins are of the thermosetting type. That is, they will cure at room temperature, although there are advantages in final strength to post-curing vinylester resins at higher temperatures.

Laminate Schedules

The laminate schedule, which determines the thickness of a hull, is generally the province of the designer and the builder, who must consider the size and intended use of the boat. Hull thicknesses vary from thin and lightweight for

These eight squares of mat and woven roving represent a typical fiberglass laminate with a finished thickness of approximately $^5/_{16}$ inch. Laid up in a mold, the laminate schedule reads, in order of application (left to right): gelcoat (not pictured), mat, mat, roving, mat, roving, mat, roving, mat. (from Fiberglass Boat Repair Manual, *by Allan Vaitses, International Marine, 1988)*

a coastwise cruiser/daysailer to thick and heavy for offshore use.

The fiber reinforcement materials discussed earlier, when chosen for their qualities of strength and workability in various sections of a hull and laid up on top of each other successively, form the laminate. The schedule determines the order in which they will be used, such as gelcoat first, then a layer of surfacing tissue (a low-density mat) to prevent the print-through of woven roving in the first layer. We have all seen perfectly nice, new boats with the waffle-iron pattern of the first layer of roving visible through the gelcoat. It is criminal to allow this to happen, because it is so simple to prevent.

All thermosetting resins have a setup time, and as the builders lay up a hull, it is critical that they complete their work within this time frame. If an entire layer or layers cannot be done within this *gelation* period, then it must be done in sections rather than all at once. Usually two to four layers are applied to the section being worked, with the butts or overlaps staggered from one layer to the next. The idea, insofar as possible, is to lay up successive layers wet on wet rather than wet on dry. Internal hull stringers are added before the final layer goes into the hull.

The laminate schedules for a couple of representative uncored sailboat hulls might be as follows:

- *Well-built 27-foot boat, displacement 4,000 pounds.* Gelcoat sprayed into a female mold to a thickness of $^1/_{32}$ inch, followed by a low-density layer of chopped-strand mat (CSM) or lightweight cloth to prevent print-through. Then come three or four layers of woven roving below the waterline, tapering back to two layers above the waterline; successive layers of woven roving are separated by a layer of CSM for better inter-layer bonding. The woven roving might weigh 16 to 24 ounces, and the resulting hull thickness will be about ¾ inch below the water-line, tapering to ½ inch above.

•*Heavy-displacement, 45-foot offshore sailboat, displacement 25,000 pounds.* Gelcoat and low-density surface layer of CSM as above. Fifteen or more layers of roving, with extensive use of hull stiffeners (frames, longitudinals, deck beams), which are virtually nonexistent in the 27-footer.

As mentioned, fiberglass cloth is not as much used in hull lay-up anymore as it once was. Nevertheless, it might be substituted for, say, three of the roving layers in the 45-footer, giving added strength for a given weight, and it is still sometimes used in deck molds as well as to reinforce stressed areas. A light-displacement vessel might also incorporate local reinforcements of biaxial and triaxial E- or even S-glasses to save weight without sacrificing strength.

Without dwelling on the details, it should be mentioned that building practices have perhaps as much effect on laminate integrity as the materials used. Optimum glass-to-resin ratios (both resin-starved and resin-rich

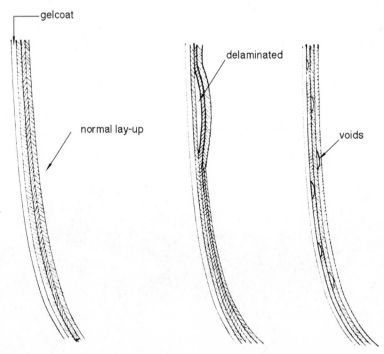

Sections through three solid-glass hull laminates, with the thickness of the layers exaggerated and the number of layers understated for clarity. In left-to-right sequence: normal lay-up; area of delamination; voids under gelcoat and in laminate. Such voids can encourage ingress of moisture and subsequent blistering (see Chapter 3).

laminates reduce strength and durability), control of contaminants in the gel-coat, thorough and even wetting out of the fiberglass, careful bonding of successive layers, and control of temperature and humidity during lay-up are among the prerequisites for a good boat. In the early years of fiberglass boatbuilding, it was common to use *chopper guns* rather than CSM. A chopper gun receives a continuous feed of strand roving, which it chops and spits out in randomly oriented short pieces entrained in a stream of catalyzed polyester resin. In skilled hands these tools can be highly effective, but proper adjustment of glass-to-resin ratios and application thickness are critical and difficult. They were frequently misused, often in cheaply built boats that had insufficient hull stiffeners. Chopper guns received so much bad press that their use these days is limited, but even the highest-quality builders still keep them around to reach such out-of-the-way places as the inside corners of deck molds and the keel cavities of internally ballasted boats.

Many boatbuilders nowadays use an impregnator, a machine that metes out resin in preset quantities and wets out the fabric before it goes into the hull mold to be rolled or squeegeed. This system adds speed and provides precise control over glass-to-resin ratios.

This machine, common today in larger boatbuilding shops, distributes resin equally over the mat or woven rovings, which can be cut to size and laid up in the mold. This makes for better quality control than wetting out the fabric after it is laid up inside the mold.

Cored Hulls and Decks

We core hulls to save weight without losing strength, to add stiffness, and to reduce the cost of construction. Not a bad combination at all. And we core decks for much the same reasons—to save weight topsides while adding load strength.

U.S. boatbuilders had been constructing solid-laminate hulls for about 12 or 13 years before a Canadian company introduced the benefits of balsa core, and in the process made itself a household word in the yacht-building industry. That company was C & C Yachts. Balsa had long been used as a deck stiffener, and it readily lent itself to use as a full or partial core for a hull. When this type of hull first appeared, the balsa was generally 1 inch thick, sandwiched between two conventional polyester resin–reinforced fiberglass *skins*, which were about ⅜ to ⁷⁄₁₆ inch thick. The laminating process was done without the benefit of any vacuum-bagging (a means of distributing even pressure over a lamination by covering the surface with plastic and sucking air out with a vacuum pump), and the skin-to-core bonds were achieved at a normal thermosetting (68 degrees F) temperature. No high-technology glasses were used—just stranded E-glass in layers of chopped-strand mat and woven rovings to achieve the skin thicknesses desired.

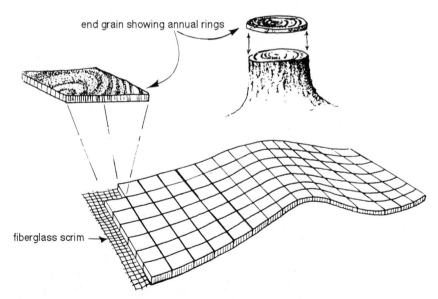

End-grain balsa core material. In the Baltek Corporation's Contourkore, end-grain panels are cut into 1-inch by 2-inch squares and glued to a loosely woven fiberglass scrim. (from *Fiberglass Boat Repair Manual,* by Allan Vaitses, International Marine, 1988)

When cores have a problem, it generally begins at the bonding surface between the core and the skin. The root of the problem is shearing stress, which causes delamination (separation) along this interface. This compromises the fundamental strength of the hull, and subsequent repairs are difficult and costly. Better-quality glass (notably S-glass), the development of vinylester and epoxy resins, and the widespread use of vinylester resin and vacuum-bagging among production builders beginning in the mid-1980s have made the art of hull coring far more dependable.

Cored Hulls

The advantages of hull cores, aside from the weight and cost savings, are increased insulation, a reduction of noise, and, maybe most important, an increase in stiffness. The core's stiffening reduces the necessary number of transverse and longitudinal stiffeners, which increases the volume in the cabin.

We do not generally core small hulls, as the weight of a solid laminate doesn't become a factor until considerable thickness of hull is necessary. There are exceptions (the J-22, the Rob Roy 23, the Nimbles, etc.), but generally speaking it is not necessary to add core for a weight advantage until a hull reaches about 30 feet, or unless some special benefit is desired—such as the excellent impact resistance of balsa or Airex.

For expediency, we will focus our discussion of cores on the main ones: balsa, polyvinyl chloride (PVC) foam (Airex is the best known), and PVC/polyurethane foam (such as Klegecell, Divinycell, and Termanto). Others, such as honeycomb cores of various materials, have been used in exotic, expensive one-off construction, but balsa and foam dominate the production boats of today.

End-grain balsa is cheaper than foam, yet has excellent stiffness and compressive strength. Its use as a core in fiberglass boats was widespread by the late 1960s or early 1970s. Given this headstart and its undeniable advantages, balsa remains the most common core. It is the core of choice in the very successful J-boats (J-24, J-35, J-37, etc.) built by Tillotson Pearson, as well as the boats of C & C, Tartan, Freedom, Hunter, and others. While balsa has much to recommend it in the way of impact strength, shear strength, and ease of working in a mold, it does have a greater risk of absorbing moisture and suffering consequent rot given any crack in the overlying laminate. If it is vacuum-bagged and bonded with epoxy or vinylester resins, this risk can be reduced considerably, but this is not always the case in production boats.

One of the objectives of this book is to enable you to recognize when a fiberglass boat is, practically speaking, "dead." Well, a balsa-cored hull that

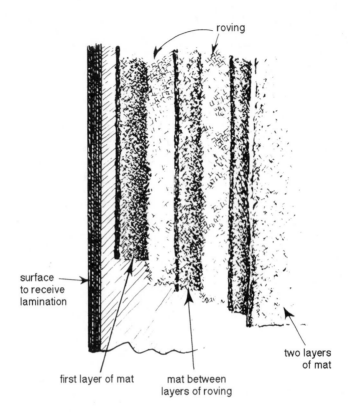

roving

surface
to receive
lamination

two layers
of mat

first layer of mat

mat between
layers of roving

A typical lay-up of the outer skin protecting a core. The outer skin is typically a bit thicker than the inner and of course includes the gelcoat surface. Mat is used between each roving layer for its better surface bonding. (from *Fiberglass Boat Repair Manual,* by Allan Vaitses, International Marine, 1988)

indicates water saturation on more than 35 percent of the hull surface and the attendant delamination of the skin-to-core bond would fit the bill. If this sounds like a condemnation of balsa as a core material below the waterline, it probably is! Unless built with great care, boats with balsa-cored under-bodies have a much shorter and more predictable lifespan than do solid laminate and Airex-cored hulls. Nevertheless, balsa makes a fine core material for topsides.

Rigid-elastic non-cross-linked pure PVC foam, better known under the brand name Airex, came to boatbuilding somewhat after balsa; the Palmer Johnson Standfast 36s of the early 1970s were among the first boats to use it. In my opinion, Airex is superior to balsa as a hull underbody core. It is more expensive, but it is well worth the increased cost. Its great advantage over balsa is its excellent resistance to rot when water does penetrate the skin. The

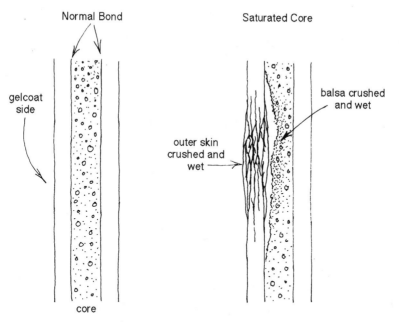

Normal Bond — Saturated Core

gelcoat side

outer skin crushed and wet

balsa crushed and wet

core

Normal bond of inner and outer skins to core (left) versus an outer-skin bond (right) that has been compromised by a substantial impact or shearing stress to the hull or deck. The crushed and delaminated outer skin has admitted water to the core, which, if balsa, may be locally saturated.

absence of cross-linking makes it highly flexible to bending and compression, which means it can absorb impacts and return to shape—a quality appreciated by anyone who has been on the rocks as many times as I have!

The cross-linked blended PVC/ polyurethane foams (such as Klegecell and Divinycell) are stiffer than Airex, but also much less flexible and more brittle. Depending on the qualities one desires, flexibility or stiffness, one can choose either form or a combination of the two. Cross-linked PVC is used, for example, in the Taylor 41 and other custom or semicustom out-and-out racers where

Core foams, deeply scored to take compound curvatures. The core material is pressed into the wet mat with weights. For sharp curves the scores would be placed on top. (from Fiberglass Boat Repair Manual, *by Allan Vaitses, International Marine, 1988)*

15

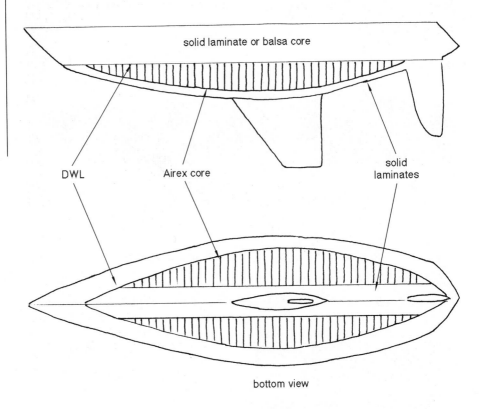

solid laminate or balsa core

DWL

Airex core

solid
laminates

bottom view

Two views of a hull showing possible combinations of cores and solid laminate. The area near the keel and hull centerline is solid fiberglass. Airex core is used around this, below the designed waterline. Above the waterline, a balsa core is a stiff, strong, cost-effective alternative.

ultimate hull stiffness and strength-to-weight ratios are desired. It is also used to save weight in the ends of some boats. Its shear strength is better than Airex but not as good as balsa. Cross-linked PVC foams bond well with nearly all resin systems.

As I mentioned, one of the principal advantages of cores is weight reduction. Of the three cores, balsa is the least efficient in this regard. It absorbs a great deal of resin, and it does so unevenly, making the bond to the fiberglass uneven. This is not normally a problem with Airex.

Honeycomb cores (of a variety of materials from aramid paper to aluminum) are the lightest of all, but given the hexagonal shape of their cells and the small bonding surface area, great care is necessary to get a good bond. High-density resins are usually used to accomplish this. Aluminum honeycomb has

16

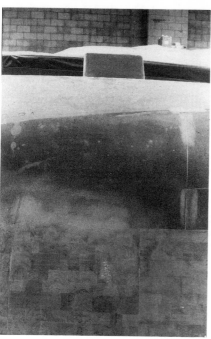

The Taylor 41, a semicustom racing hull, shows very advanced use of composite building materials. The hull is solid glass at the keel centerline, and the bottom uses Airex core. The ends topside use Divinycell to save weight, and finally the topsides at the rail have balsa core for high impact strength. The core materials are not combined; rather, each is used for a specific property—light weight, compression strength, impact strength, etc.

far better compression and shear strength than paper. Honeycomb's high cost has so far made it feasible only in custom boats, primarily racing powerboats and sailboats. Perhaps it will gain greater acceptance as price and the ability of builders to work it improve, but I do worry about the small contact surface and the skill necessary to build with it. It is difficult to envision honeycomb being used in production building anytime in the foreseeable future.

Cored-hull construction must revert to solid laminate at a keel stubby or at the hull centerline.

Cored Decks

The two most recurring problem areas I deal with on condition surveys are decks and rudders. Decks are more serious, because they contribute to the overall strength of a boat, much like the top of an I-beam. The cost of repairing a fully deteriorated deck can exceed the value of a 15-year-old boat, making it a total constructive loss, or virtually worthless.

The deck core of choice has been balsa for many years, and it is likely to remain so, due only in part to low cost. Balsa's good compression strength and light weight offer the same advantages in a deck as in a hull. You might think that being out of the water most of the time would make cored decks relatively free of problems, but that is not the case. Too often, thin cores (less than ¾ inch) are used between very thin skins. The result is a weak platform that begins to flex almost from day one, with nothing more than normal foot traffic on the foredeck, trunk cabin, or side decks. The light hulls and insufficient hull stiffeners of many small boats, combined with a flexible deck, don't like a lot of stress, and boats are subject to constant stress—sometimes in tension, compression, and torsion simultaneously.

Given these stresses, a lightweight deck is going to delaminate in a short time. The deck also will develop stress cracks from the constant flexing, and this allows moisture to get at the core. Added to these problems are the many holes in a deck to mount stanchions, rails, hawsepipes, and chainplates—all of which are subject to leaking if not properly bedded and kept tightened.

I have surveyed decks on some of the old Hood/Maas 50s that were nearly 20 years old and in near-perfect condition. The cores were 2-inch balsa between very substantial skins, reinforced with stringers under the deck in high-stress areas. On the other hand, I have surveyed 0'Day 30s whose decks were almost totally delaminated after 10 years. These cores were ¾-inch balsa between thin skins and didn't have any reinforcing stringers under the decks.

Airex is less often used as a deck core. In addition to being more expensive than balsa, it used to have a tendency to become spongy underfoot in hot climates, though I am told this problem has been overcome.

The rigidity of the cross-linked PVC foams is certainly a desirable attribute for a deck, but their expense limits their use in production boatbuilding. Foam-cored decks are lighter than their balsa-cored counterparts and won't rot when the core gets wet. Properly installed, however, both balsa and cross-linked PVC make excellent deck cores.

Whichever core material you find or choose, keep in mind that good construction and design will make any core relatively safe. Vacuum-bagging the

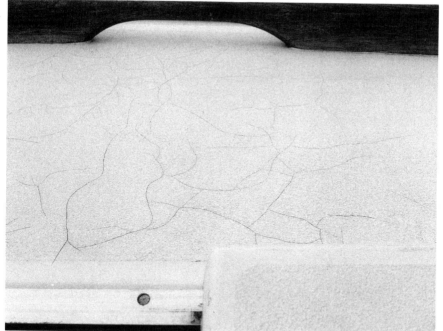

Crazing in the cabintop of a C & C 24-footer. This area is directly over the half-bulkhead separating the semi-enclosed toilet compartment from the main cabin, and receives heavy traffic when the mainsail is furled. Flexing over the bulkhead may have caused the crazing, which in this case is not merely cosmetic; water has gotten at the underlying balsa core, and humps in the surface (not visible here) indicate local core saturation, as did the moisture meter. A thorough fix would call for cutting away the upper skin over the affected area (an inner fiberglass liner obstructs access from underneath), digging out the damaged core, laying down new core and laminating a new outer skin with epoxy resin, then fairing with epoxy putty. Alternatively, it would be possible to bond the old skin to the new core, or not to remove the skin at all, instead injecting epoxy resin into the core through drilled holes and weighting or clamping down the skin to renew the skin-core bond. In any case, the last step should probably be to grind and refinish this entire 16-year-old deck, renewing the nonskid either with a paint additive or commercially available nonskid panels that are glued down with epoxy. (Photo courtesy Jonathan Eaton)

skin-to-core bond will help. In addition, epoxy or vinylester resins will give greater bonding strengths than polyesters, and the thickness of the core material will affect the overall strength of the deck platform. Cored-deck construction should revert to solid laminate near the hull-deck joint, along sharp-radius curves such as those from deck to cabin sides, near chainplates, and where any highly stressed deck hardware is through-fastened.

Chapter 2

Stresses and Strains

The first procedure in my surveys is a leisurely walk around the hull and deck to spot any obvious flaws, which would include grounding damage below the waterline, keel problems, rudder problems, and so forth. In particular, stress lines or cracks tell the surveyor a great deal about a boat's condition. These may appear on decks, trunk cabins, topsides and bottoms, keel reinforcements, and transoms, and around deck fittings, chainplates, hull stringers, ports, and hatches. Some, as you will see, have considerably more consequence than others. Since stress cracks and blisters are the most visible symptoms of deterioration of fiberglass boats, this chapter and the one following examine them in detail. With these subjects out of the way, we'll be able to move through the boat survey procedures more efficiently, beginning in Chapter 4.

Stress Indicators

There are so many variable forces at work at any one time on a boat: structural members and panels that are sometimes in *compression*, sometimes in *tension*, other times in *torsion*, sometimes subjected to *shearing* stress and strain, and most of the time subject to all of these forces simultaneously. A careful interpretation of stress indications inside and outside a hull will tell you where weaknesses, if any, are located, and more often than not what caused them. The trick is to determine whether common stress has progressed far enough to change the shape of a hull or deck, thereby degrading its structural effectiveness in future service.

A lack of panel stiffness in hulls and decks is the primary reason why stresses and strains cause damage. The size and intended use of a boat have a lot to do with how much reinforcement is designed into it. Smaller production cruising boats (less than 26 to 28 feet) and daysailers rarely have many stringers for longitudinal support or bulkheads and floors for transverse support, and their hulls are not as strong or stiff because the laminate is thinner and usually isn't cored. These boats, when used on lakes, bays, and other sheltered waters, do not ordinarily suffer premature or excessive stress-induced problems. On the ocean, however, they are subject to the same physical forces as larger craft, and would need to be stiffer to stay healthy over the long haul. This is not a blanket condemnation of the seaworthiness of small boats: A small boat can be as stiff and strong as its larger brethren, but the market forces driving the mass production of small boats rarely permit this.

Panel Stiffness

To increase the stiffness of a hull or deck panel of given thickness, you simply reduce the spans of unsupported laminate. Imagine, for the sake of argument, a molded hull with nothing inside it. To stiffen it, a combination of longitudinal and transverse reinforcements are laminated into the hull shell. Bulkheads and floors give most of the transverse support, and full-length hull stringers provide longitudinal stiffness. The finished system looks like a grid. Cored hulls are inherently stiffer than uncored hulls, and therefore generally require fewer interior stiffeners.

If the hull isn't thick enough or is inadequately stiffened, it will deflect when force is applied, whether from a seaway or even a jackstand support while in storage.

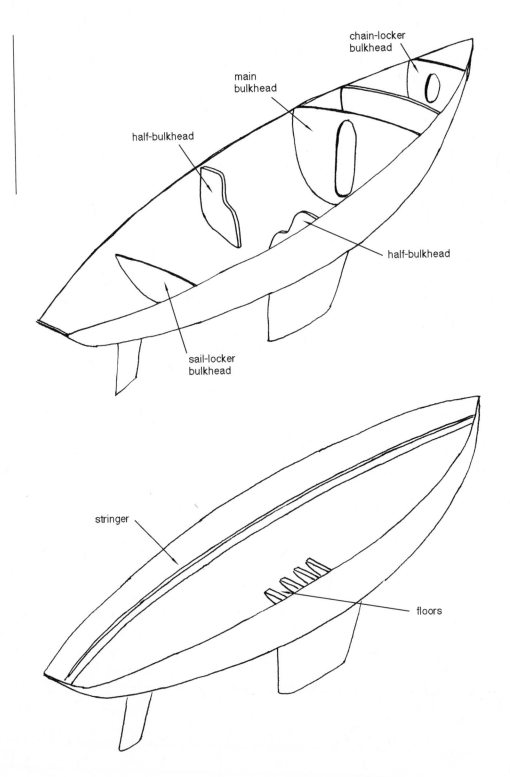

chain-locker
bulkhead

main
bulkhead

half-bulkhead

half-bulkhead

sail-locker
bulkhead

stringer

floors

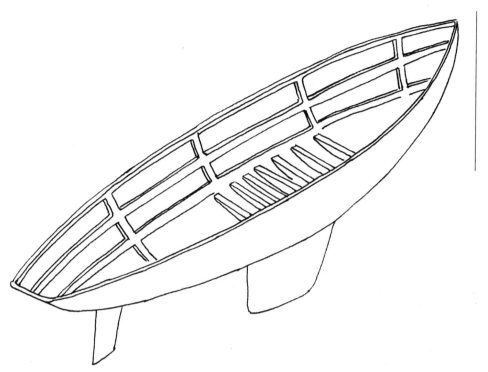

The first of these simplified hulls (top left) *relies only on bulkheads for stiffening. This is insufficient, and will probably lead to undue flexing of the hull. The second hull* (bottom left) *supplements the bulkheads (omitted for clarity) with several short floors over the keel and a single longitudinal stringer on each side. The third example (bulkheads again omitted) has three longitudinals per side, full frames, and large floors. This extremely stiff, strong construction is represented by the Swans, among others.*

Deck Stress

Cracks around lifeline stanchion bases result from local loads, such as a heavy crewmember falling against the stanchion. The gelcoat surface has cracked because there is inadequate support under the stanchion base. Installing a backing plate or block under the deck at the base of the stanchion allows the laminate to dissipate this type of stress with less probability of damage. Builders should bring a deck core no closer than about 5 inches from the edge of the deck, so that the hull-deck joint (which, hopefully, is through-bolted), will be made in solid laminate. To do otherwise is to increase the likelihood of moisture getting in and/or delamination of the core bond.

For most of the same reasons, coring should be avoided under such high-

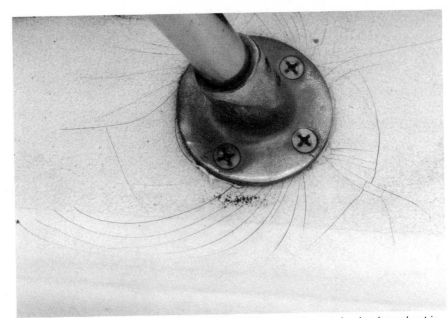

Crazing of a deck around a stanchion base. This stanchion angles backward yet is not supported by a forward-angled strut, as it probably should be. Furthermore, it is located where it will be grabbed for support by anyone boarding from a dinghy, and leaned on by anyone lounging on deck beside the cockpit. Finally, there is no backing block or plate belowdeck. Years of insults have taken their toll. Solution: Glass-in a large backing block under the deck, then rebed the baseplate in poly-sulfide adhesive sealant and refasten through the block. That will stabilize the area. The damage, which in this case is cosmetic, can be fixed now or when the deck is refinished. (Photo courtesy Jonathan Eaton)

stress hardware as genoa tracks and the exit holes for the chainplates. These two areas in particular develop some serious tension from the rigging and the loaded genoa sheets. The chance of delamination of the core material is too great, and these sections should be solid laminate glass with plenty of "beef" in the glass.

Decks with inadequate core thickness and an absence of reinforcing members are vulnerable both to localized stress and to flexural stresses over a wider area, running transversely or fore and aft. If you see a great number of long stress cracks, probably the deck has been flexing underfoot. It indicates that the platform was undersized to begin with.

Decks have many contours in the mold, and a good deal of chopped-strand mat is used in the laminate schedules, because it is easier to work into tight corners. But strength is also needed in the form of cloth weave, either

E-glass or S-glass, and where core is used it must be of adequate thickness—ideally at least 1 inch in the case of balsa, although ¾ inch is the norm and ½ inch is common on smaller boats. Too many builders try to get structural performance out of a total sandwich thickness of 1 inch (two ¼-inch skins and ½ inch of balsa core). The boat must carry crew who weigh the same as those on a larger vessel, and is subject to the same sea conditions during coastal use.

A long crack across a deck is probably a result of the deck surface flexing over a fixed bulkhead, such as a chain locker. The narrower, triangulated surface of the deck at the bow may be strong enough, but farther aft, the larger surface may crack because it is unsupported except by the bulkhead, over which it flexes and hinges.

I sometimes see long stress cracks in the deck running close inside the toerails, roughly from the stem aft some 3 to 6 feet. There are several explanations for this type of damage. One is the sharp-radiused angle in the molding in those boats in which the deck edge turns upward into the inner face of the toerail. Where CSM was used as a first layer of reinforcement and was not tightly rolled out next to the gelcoat, this causes a weakness, and allows minor hull flexing to crack the gelcoat surface along this section. However, this type of

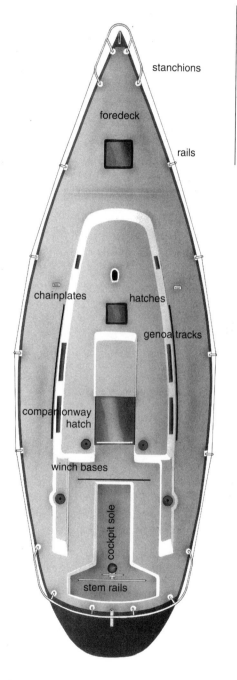

A boat's deck is susceptible to stress in a variety of locations, highlighted here. (Illustration by Henry Hill)

hull-deck joint is not common anymore. Another possibility is that the mid-section of the foredeck is flexing enough to cause some hinge cracking in this area. A hinge-type crack would normally be somewhat deeper, and probably read higher on a moisture meter, the use of which I will detail later.

Other common locations of stress cracks on deck include the corners of the trunk cabin where it joins the foredeck, and sometimes all the way around the base of the trunk cabin. More often than not these are cosmetic stresses caused by poor mating of the underlying mat layer to the gelcoat, making the gelcoat try to perform as a strength member, which it is not. The corners of the cockpit where the coamings join the deckhouse present the same problem. Look for stress cracks around the edges of any hatches on deck—these also are caused by poor reinforcement and roll-out technique.

Mast collars for keel-stepped masts need to be well reinforced, and I see too much core in this area of many boats. If a stayed mast is wedged in place properly, in theory only modest pressure should be exerted on the collars. Today, however, many cruising sailboats use hydraulic backstays. These, while intended to rake the mast, also exert pressure on the collar, and if the collar sections are not well reinforced, stress damage may result. Because the collar is nothing other than a hole in the deckhouse, it is prone to leaks in the boot and down the spar's luff channel, both of which can cause moisture to penetrate and weaken the surrounding laminates, especially in any areas of exposed balsa core. Several building practices will keep this area strong. The

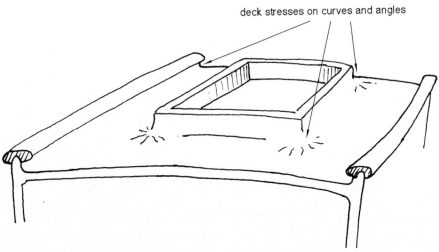

deck stresses on curves and angles

Crazing is common along tight-radius curves, as where a deck turns up into bulwarks or hatch coamings.

first is to build up solid laminate around the opening; the second is to install a cast aluminum insert that covers the exposed laminate and has a flange that is bedded on deck. Finally, when the rig is tall, the builder can install a tie-bar alongside the mast between the step and the deck. This tie-bar keeps the deck from flexing up and down when the mast pumps and thereby being gradually weakened. Owners need to make every effort to keep this area as dry as possible by filling the unused section of the mast channel with clear caulking and keeping the collar area tightly covered.

Deck-stepped masts allow more room belowdecks, but they also impose a major stress on deck that must be adequately absorbed and dissipated. Frequently a vertical member, sometimes called a *compression post*, is used to transfer the load from the deck step plate to the keel. This might be a wood cornerpost on the inboard edge of a main bulkhead, or a small-diameter steel or aluminum strut set directly under the step.

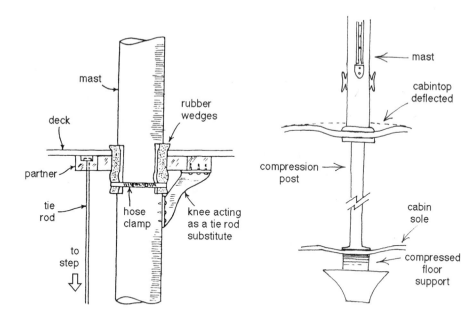

One way to stop the pumping of a keel-stepped mast from flexing the deck is to fasten a tie rod between the mast partners and the step. (from *Understanding Rigs and Rigging,* by Richard Henderson, International Marine, 1991)

This is what can happen when there is insufficient athwartship landing for the compression post under a deck-stepped mast.

Alternatively, some deck steps are supported by an athwartship beam—often of laminated hardwood and usually incorporated into the main bulkhead. This might also be tabbed to the overhead with fiberglass reinforcements.

The most common problem with deck steps is that the compression post is not well supported in the keel area, and therefore starts "sinking" with age. This in turn permits the step area to sag downward, cracking the deck gelcoat as well as the overhead liner in the cabin. The shrouds may loosen, and if the owner tightens the shrouds without noticing the root problem, the condition will only worsen.

The base of the compression post must be firmly supported by a transverse member that distributes the stress athwartships. If the post merely sits on the keel ballast, it could potentially drive the ballast out of the boat. Furthermore, if the deck is cored, it should revert to solid laminate under the step. By inspecting the deck surfaces around the step for signs of crazing, and then, in the cabin, examining the overhead around the step and the area in the bilge where the compression is being exerted, you can fairly easily locate any problems with a deck-stepped mast.

In evaluating common stress cracks on decks, keep in mind that some light surface crazing is fairly common on nearly all boats. If it is not deep into the gelcoat surface, the structural implications are minor. If the cracks are open and deep, moisture is reaching the core bond within the deck, with repercussions ranging from flexing of the deck to a loss of structural integrity. When a large section of a foredeck begins to flex, so do the hull-to-deck flanges and the sides of the hull as well. The first thing a delaminated deck wants to do is swell upward as moisture gets under the gelcoat or into the core. These raised or swelled areas can be felt by hand. The use of a small tapping hammer will tell the surveyor if separation is present at the core bond, and judicious use of a moisture meter should confirm the presence of greater amounts of moisture in the stressed areas. (The surveyor's tools are discussed in Chapter 4.)

A good test of a deck is simply to walk on it. Any deflection of the surface, crunching noise, or water seeping from a stress crack will indicate some fairly serious problems. On the other hand, the more a surveyor can see of a deck, the better an evaluation he can make. On some boats, access to the underside of the deck is very good, because overhead panels can be easily removed for inspection. On others, the overhead is fixed and no inspection can be made. Full fiberglass liners, popular nowadays with some of the bigger production builders for their role as positive structural elements when epoxied to the hull, make inspection of any hull difficult. It seems true that good builders make access easy, and the lower down the quality scale you travel, the less you can view.

Rig-Related Deck Stresses

Stresses around genoa tracks, chainplates, backstays, and mast collar sections are all tension generated. Most chainplate installations consist of flat bar or rod led through the deck to fiberglass-covered plywood knees, which are then fiberglassed to the side of the hull or through-bolted to fixed structural bulkheads. Backstays are led through the deck to a piece of flat stainless steel laid along the outside surface of the transom, reinforced with a backing plate, and bolted in place. Headstay chainplates are generally integral with the stemhead fitting and also through-bolted to the stem.

Prior to 1975, most sailboat designs used separate chainplates for the lower and upper shrouds. Three separate knees/bulkheads handled the rigging loads and distributed them along the deck surface. Current designs often use a single chainplate that accommodates the uppers and the lowers. How well this single plate is anchored inside the hull will determine how much ten-

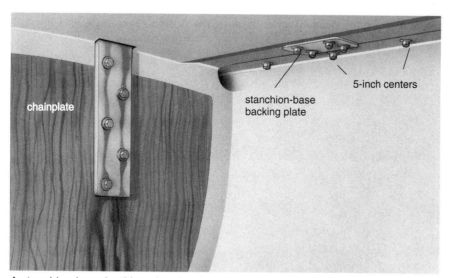

A stanchion-base backing plate installed belowdeck will eliminate stress cracking imposed by local loads. Note also the stainless steel machine bolts, on approximately 5-inch centers, sealing the hull-to-deck joint. Deck stress at the chainplates causes bedding seals to loosen, resulting in interior leaks. (Illustration by Henry Hill)

sion is generated on the deck surface. These stresses generally will occur in one of two ways: The chainplate may be pulled upward through the deck, or the deck itself will be pulled upward and distorted. Both problems invariably lead to leaks through the chainplate relief holes, which become elongated by the stress. I use a batten laid flat along the deck surface to determine if deflection exists around all the chainplates, then I check for stress cracks, measure the moisture content, and do a percussion test to see if any delaminations are present.

Strengthening the knee or the interior structural member holding the chainplate in place belowdecks will solve this type of problem. I have rarely seen problems related to good-size knees supporting chainplate installations. I have occasionally seen light bulkheads holding a chainplate

A chainplate on a J-30, showing the effects of poor bedding on deck. Leaks through the deck have stained the bulkhead. Notice how the top of the main bulkhead is fully tabbed (bonded) to the underside of the deck, a desirable characteristic on any boat.

be pulled off their tabbings. Most often, problems develop when the chainplate is through-bolted to the back of a berth that runs longitudinally between the main bulkhead and the partial bulkhead for a galley or nav station. In this type of installation—widely used in modern construction—the idea is that the I-beam between the bulkheads can sustain the tension loads. The method does work, but only if all the structural members involved are good-sized, the longitudinal member is fiberglassed to the hull and the deck, and the bonds to each bulkhead are strong. If light materials and poor bonding exist, there will be movement of all the components, which in turn is transmitted to the deck.

Backstays, considering the tension loads they take (especially when fitted with hydraulic tensioning rams), seem often to be underreinforced. Transom laminates of production boats are pretty thin, and if a very large interior backing plate isn't fitted, the chances of pulling the after quarter of the boat out of shape are good. This type of stress usually manifests itself by pulling the chain-

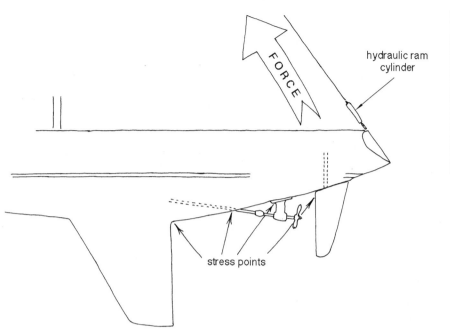

FORCE

hydraulic ram
cylinder

stress points

*Excessive backstay tension can cause a hull to develop a transverse crack between
the end of the keel and the strut bearing, and the rudder and/or shaft to bind.*

plate upward and causing stress cracks on the exterior gelcoat, both on deck
and on the transom; it can be accompanied by leaking through the plate relief
hole. In extreme cases, the tension is so great that a transverse crack several
inches long will develop across the underbody, between the end of the keel and
the strut bearing. This type of strain—which is peculiar to the flat-bottom, fin-
keel, spade-rudder hull style and can bind the rudder or the propeller shaft—
will show abaft the keel when a vessel is being surveyed "rig in" and the backstay is loaded to 1,500 pounds or so. In any event, when a backstay chainplate
is through-bolted and a backing plate fitted, the entire fabrication should be
encased in fiberglass so that it becomes integral with the transom.

Genoa tracks are too frequently attached over cored sections of the deck,
because this is thought to offer good stiffness. I don't advise it. The large head-
sails used today exert tremendous pressure on the tracks, and the flexing is
likely to delaminate the core bond and cause leaks into the quarter berth, plus
a gradual weakening of the deck and deterioration of the core from moisture. It is better to use solid laminate, very well reinforced under the deck with
a stainless steel flat bar of $3/16$- to $1/4$-inch thickness (or hardwood or aluminum
of equivalent strength) and the same width as the genoa track.

Headstays, while they fail as much as or more than any other component of the standing rigging, do not normally show much stress on decks. This is because they are mounted at a very heavily reinforced section of the boat, namely the stem.

The Hull-Deck Joint

The cornerstone of a strong deck is the hull-to-deck joint. Whether it is an inner flange, an outer lip flange, or a vertical flange, the important thing is that it be through-bolted on 5- to 7-inch centers, normally with stainless steel machine bolts. The inner flange method, which laps the deck mold over the flange, allows the caprail to become integral with the joint and affords a solid and generally watertight seal if the caulking holds up. On cruising boats, this rail can be used to attach a sheeting block for genoas, whereas a more performance-oriented boat needs the tracks brought inboard for better sheeting angles. Whichever method is used, the deck flange must be of good size and strength and should be adequately thick to resist flexing and hinge cracking. Too many sailboats in the 32- to 40-foot range use self-tapping screws to secure the deck to the hull flange. This is not suitable for an offshore yacht.

A good boat will give you access to the hull-to-deck joint for a view, and you can readily see what the builder used to fasten the deck, at what intervals, and also the thickness and depth of the hull flange.

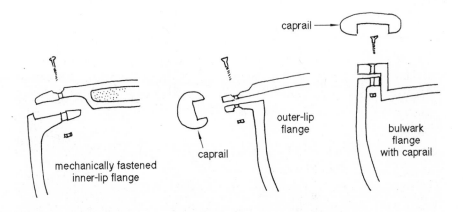

caprail

mechanically fastened
inner-lip flange

caprail

outer-lip
flange

bulwark
flange
with caprail

Three common hull-deck joints. Look for cracks in the flanges, adequate through-bolts, extra strength in the laminations at the join, and adequate bedding between the flanges.

Hull Stresses—Rail to Ballast Keel

Now we come to an important difference between fiberglass construction and that of steel, aluminum, or wood. Boats built of metal or wood are plated or planked from stock of a specified and uniform thickness, say ⅜-inch plate or 1-inch planking. In fiberglass construction, especially since the early 1980s, the hull laminates are generally thinner above the waterline than they are below. So, an uncored hull that may be 1 to 1½ inches thick near the keel may taper to ½ inch at the waterline and ¼ inch or less at the rail. This is not ideal, because a strong hull flange is needed in the hull-deck joint to absorb deck stresses.

Some problems associated with this type of hull construction arise from the sections of unsupported fiberglass panels above the waterline and between the bow and the main structural bulkheads. On a typical 36- to 40-foot yacht, this span is some 10 to 12 feet long and 4 feet or so high, and its only support may be provided by the edges of the V-berths, which are supposed to act as fore-and-aft reinforcing stringers between the main bulkhead and the chain locker bulkhead. While this is intended to stiffen the entire forward section of the vessel, it isn't enough. On a wooden or steel hull of similar size there are frames every 8 to 9 inches on center, and longitudinal stringers running fore and aft on roughly 2-foot centers. The effect is a gridlike reinforcement of the hull shell. In fiberglass boats, large sections of unsupported panels will "oil can," or flex, in moderate to heavy sea conditions.

As the hull flexes, cracks can develop on the exterior gelcoat around the only rigid interior reinforcements, the V-berth stringers and the main bulkhead. The cracks along the berth stringers are both compressive and tensile;

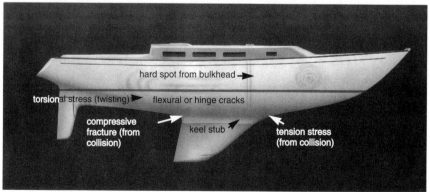

Profile of a typical cruising sailboat showing areas susceptible to stress damage. (Illustration by Henry Hill)

the outside of the hull is pushed inward in compression, while the interior laminate is stretched in tension. This is what causes hinge cracks in a hull, and they can be very destructive to the integrity of the fiberglass. Once the gelcoat is breached, moisture starts seeping into the laminate, and ultimately the hull itself will be compromised.

The other stress point susceptible to hull flexing is at the main bulkhead, which separates the forward cabin from the main cabin. Here, cracks in the fiberglass can appear over the hard spot where the bulkhead is tabbed to the inside of the hull. Eventually this action will strain the fiberglass tabs holding the bulkhead in place.

If the vessel under survey is intended for offshore use, pronounced cracks in either of these two places should certainly cause it to fail survey.

Unsupported panels in other sections of the hull may not show any signs of stress because they do not suffer the continuous pounding that the bow sections do. Nevertheless, the area aft of the half bulkheads that separate the galley or nav station from the main cabin, and extending to the transom, is also vulnerable. The only panel reinforcement here may be the small bulkhead at the forward end of a cockpit sail locker, and many boats less than 30 feet long do not even have the transverse stiffening of a bridge deck. Without

In this design, typical of cruising sailboats under 30 feet, only a fiberglass sill separates the companionway opening from the cockpit well. A bridge deck across the forward end of the cockpit would provide stiffness and guard against downflooding should the cockpit be swamped, but the bridge deck is usually omitted on small boats, where space is at a premium. (Photo courtesy Jonathan Eaton)

adequate stiffening aft, the hull cannot adequately resist or absorb backstay tension or torsional stresses.

The resultant working can cause crescent-shaped stress cracks along the boat's quarter panels, usually on both sides. Hulls suffering from this weakness frequently are difficult to support out of the water, as well. You see them on jackstands in the boatyards with the forward and after panels deflected under the poppets.

Keel Stress

We use two basic keels: internal and external. External keels are lead or iron appendages attached to the hull with stainless or galvanized steel bolts—generally stainless in a lead keel and galvanized in iron. Lead and stainless make the more desirable combination, lasting longer. Many European and English builders still persist in using iron keels unless the buyer specifies lead. Iron pits and degenerates rapidly in salt water, unless it is sheathed in fiberglass or coated with epoxy sealants, and it has to be continuously maintained.

Galvanized bolts and iron keels will continue to be used in smaller craft, but keep in mind that galvanized keel bolts will probably last no longer than 15 to 20 years, whereas quality stainless will last roughly twice as long.

Keels are subject to all forms of stress, so of course they have to be very well attached to the hull. Early fiberglass boats designed to the CCA (Cruising Club of America) rules used a keel very similar to those on wooden boats, which is to say the ballast was a relatively small casting attached to the base of the keel "stump," which was

A keelbolt and floor on a J-29. The external lead ballast is bolted through a molded keel stump, or stubby. Early models of this boat used vermiculite-filled putty around the bolt heads, but this was too brittle and sometimes cracked after a grounding, which allowed water to leak up past the keelbolts into the bilge.

part of the molded hull and very strong. With the widespread adoption of the fin keel in the 1970s, things became more complex. Keels were suddenly deeper with a higher aspect ratio; they had less bearing surface for the attachment, and they were subjected to more torsional stress. C & C Yachts was one of the early firms to address this problem successfully. C & C used a large molded keel stump, or "stubby," that extended some 12 inches below the bottom of the hull. The cast lead keel sections were fitted to the stump, and the bolts led through the stump to the bilge, where they were fitted with large nuts. The bolts into the lead were tapped and also fitted with retaining nuts. The joint between the lead and the fiberglass was filled with polysulfide, and the bolts were then snugged up. This was, and is, a great keel-to-hull joint. It is strong and can take a hell of a whack on the lead without damaging the centerline structure of the hull. It is also relatively easy to repair any damage to the external lead.

In the 1980s, designers drew flatter bottom sections and shallower bilges, and very thin interior floor supports were the result. Keels became thinner and deeper, as much as 8 to 9 feet deep. More of the stump was removed, and in some cases it was removed entirely, with the ballast bolted flush to the bottom of the boat. Now the problem became (and still is) one of even greater lateral area on the ballasted fin combined with less bearing surface; the thin design of these keels makes it difficult to install enough keelbolts, and they are sometimes very short bolts. An example of this type of configuration is the Frers 41.

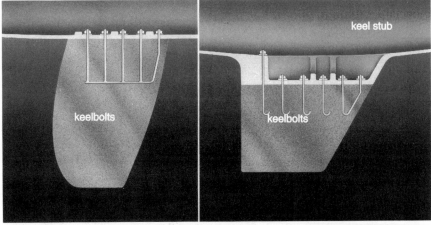

Two types of attachments for external fin keels: The lead fin bolted onto the bottom of a dedicated keel stub is an excellent method for cruising boats. Due to the flat deadrise, the elliptical flush-mounted fin is difficult to support adequately. (Illustrations by Henry Hill)

It should be emphasized that serious racing sailors are often willing to compromise strength for speed, but cruising and offshore sailors ought not to. If you ground a boat with a flat bottom, small interior floor supports, and a keel of this deep, elliptical design, you are going to damage the center-line structure. The repair, in most cases, will be very expensive. The same grounding on a stub-mounted keel might result in nothing more than a good gouge to the external lead.

In evaluating the condition of the keel, there are several places to focus your attention. The first is the exterior condition of the lead. In other words, does the boat "know" every rock on the Eastern Seaboard? Is there evidence of previous repairs? The second area to inspect is the keel-to-hull joint. I am especially careful to note any sign of leakage here when the boat is hauled. Ruptures in the joint frequently cause leakage into the bilge due to elongation of the keelbolt relief holes; if water leaks in, it will also leak out. If you are in doubt about this type of damage, wait until the boat has dried out on the ways, fill up the bilge, and wait.

The next areas to inspect are the adjacent fiberglass panel sections—forward, aft, and to either side of the keel. Keels, when hit, tend to cantilever. More often than not, the blow occurs dead on or at a slight angle, transferring shock to a rigid section of the hull in a compressive force. When one finds evidence of a hard hit on the external ballast, one should immediately check the joint for leakage or misalignment and then look for previous repairs, stress cracks, or deflection in the adjacent fiberglass panels.

Further confirmation of this type of damage may be found inside the vessel in the sump or bilge area, especially at the floor hats (transverse supports in the bilge). If these have been cracked or broken, or if the tabbing is loose, there has been a very hard grounding. Frequently a gouge

Bilge floor repair to a J-29 sloop, necessitated by a hard grounding. The mat and roving tabbing of the floor hats to the hull was cracked. The new tabbing uses S-glass for its superior strength. These floors stiffen the hull and distribute the keel load to a greater area of the hull surface.

in the keel is associated with little or no other structural damage. It takes a good deal of force to damage the centerline structure in most well-constructed vessels.

Rudder Stress

A rudder, especially the spade type without skeg so popular today, is at risk in much the same way that a keel is, but with considerably less strength in the unit itself and a great deal less reinforcement around it. It may well be the *Achilles' heel* of a modern fast hull design. The only reason we put up with the damn things is the combination of high lift and low resistance, resulting in greater hull speed and acceleration. We also give up a lot.

Many stock fiberglass yachts use a tubular glass rudder sleeve that encases and holds the rudderpost in place. Encased in the stern sections, this tube runs vertically from the bottom of the hull to the deck, or somewhere above the waterline in any event. The principal method of reinforcing it is to wrap it with layers of mat and S-glass and install buttressing knees around its base. Unfortunately, the degree of reinforcement varies widely. Some tubes have no knee supports, some two, some four. The result is an appendage 5 to 9 feet long by 2 feet wide being held in place by a 2- to 3-inch stainless steel rudderpost, which runs up through a tube that may or may not have adequate strength to support it! To this post is attached the steering gear, most often in the form of a quadrant secured to the midpoint of the post.

It follows that when a fin keel grounds, the next point of impact is going to be the rudder. When unprotected spade rudders first came into widespread use, they were fairly substantial, solid fiberglass units. When they got hit, serious damage sometimes occurred to the hull at the point where the rudderpost entered the tube. Boats sometimes sank due to these accidents, or steering was lost entirely. As a result, designers began filling the rudders with injected structural foam, which lightened them considerably, and then designed an interconnected webbing of reinforcement inside the blade that extended only about two-thirds of the way down. In a grounding, the lower third of the rudder tears away, leaving enough surface area for steerage until repairs can be effected. That, at least, is the theory.

In 15 years of surveying, my inspections have turned up more problems with rudders than any other single component. Foam-cored, tear-away spade types are the worst. As I have pointed out, they are weak by design, under-reinforced inside the hull, and very prone to absorbing water through the thin

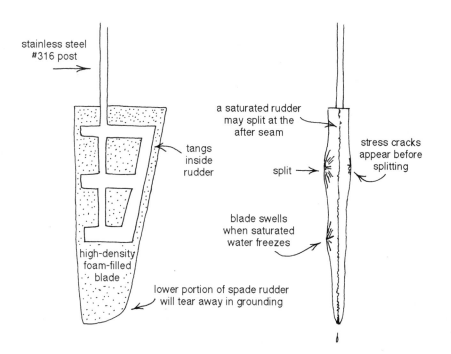

stainless steel
#316 post

a saturated rudder
may split at the
after seam

stress cracks
appear before
splitting

tangs
inside
rudder

split →

blade swells
when saturated
water freezes

high-density
foam-filled
blade

lower portion of spade rudder
will tear away in grounding

Rudders can be a problem area—particularly foam-filled "tear-away" spade rudders. When water gets inside it can freeze and expand, causing swelling, stress cracks, and even a split down the vulnerable after seam where the two halves of the shell are joined.

outer skins after even a year or two of use. They are molded in halves, joined together, and injected with foam. The skins of each half are thin, about $3/16$ inch. In cold climates, any moisture entrapped over the summer months freezes during the winter and swells the blade surface, splits the rudder down the centerline joint, or both. This happens so often that we ought to have freeze plugs to drain them after the season.

But what we really need is a better rudder, not some near throwaway type that is impossible to reinforce correctly inside the boat. The best alternative is a solid skeg protecting the rudder, even if it sacrifices optimum efficiency. I highly recommend skeg-hung rudders for cruising boats.

Internal Ballast

Some boats are built with an internally ballasted keel, as opposed to the external lead discussed earlier. The keel cavity is molded into the hull, and later the

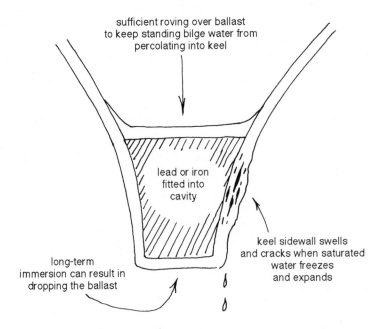

sufficient roving over ballast
to keep standing bilge water from
percolating into keel

lead or iron
fitted into
cavity

keel sidewall swells
and cracks when saturated
water freezes
and expands

long-term
immersion can result in
dropping the ballast

The effects of water on the ballast cavity of an internal keel can be devastating if the structure is compromised. In a worst-case scenario, there is a danger of "dropping" the ballast if the keel laminates fail due to long-term water damage.

ballast is dropped into the cavity and secured in place.

Internal ballast is used in many yachts produced overseas, particularly Taiwan-built boats of the 1970s and 1980s. It is common to find almost anything used as ballast in these boats—except lead! I have found cement, iron pigs and scrap metal, parts of steel reinforcing bars, scraps of train rails, and in one case what appeared to be the remnant of an old typewriter carriage. I have found some pretty unsavory things in the keels of domestic-built boats, too.

To be effective over a long period of time, internal ballast must have a very substantial thickness of glass around the cavity, including the bottom and sidewalls, and the leading and trailing edges should be especially well reinforced. Lead is the material of choice for the ballast, but you are not going to get lead in most non-U.S.-built boats; therefore, you want the iron used instead to be cast in one piece and not a conglomeration of old shell casings floating in a bath of cement. Last, the covering of fiberglass over the top of the ballast, securing it from movement, should be strong and sloped slightly aft so that water does not accumulate and leak into the ballast cavity. This area of the bilge is probably going to house waste or water and fuel tanks, so it isn't going to be very accessible. Since water impermeability is as important as strength here, the use of epoxy resins in the lay-up makes good sense. A properly angled glass seal over the ballast will direct water into the bilge sump, where it belongs.

If water is allowed to collect on the top of the ballast reinforcement, sooner or later it will penetrate, and once the reaction between the cast iron, cement, and whatever else is down there gets going, serious problems can develop, the worst of which is "dumping" the ballast out of the boat unexpectedly and capsizing.

If you are having an internally ballasted vessel surveyed, I suggest you obtain permission from the seller to have some small holes drilled into the sides of the cavity to determine what is in there, and what condition it's in.

Chapter 3

Boat Pox

I remember distinctly the early 1980s "panic" among boatowners when the blister phenomenon hit. I am talking, of course, about "boat pox"—the mysterious appearance of blisters on a boat's underbody. For a time, it was virtually impossible to get a good price for a boat with blisters, and many a sale went down the drain while the industry and surveyors tried to make some sense of the problem.

Causes

The reports I have read about osmotic blistering, including the University of Rhode Island study, the Amoco study, and others, generally focus on the chemical composition of the resins and invoke a failure of the resin systems to prevent blistering. These studies seem to suggest that better resins are the solution to the problem. I don't disagree with this thinking, but I've always wondered about the great number of boats built prior to 1980, some 23 years' worth, that have had little or no problem with blistering. What changed after 1980, if, as the resin suppliers claimed, the same resins were being used?

I've heard it suggested that resin formulations did in fact change in the early 1980s in response to petrochemical shortages, but I think the explanation is less exotic. The production boatbuilding industry of the 1950s and 1960s was small, and the number of boats being built by, say, Pearson Yachts in a year might have been 20 (my estimate). By 1982, the industry was in full bloom, and production had increased in some cases twenty-fold. Boat-building has always been a labor-intensive business, and in an effort to stem the wildly increasing prices—they rose as much as 15 to 20 percent per year for a number of years—management tried to lower costs with faster construction methods and more lightly built hulls. This meant simply using less gelcoat, less fiberglass, less core material, and fewer reinforcing members. The boats got "cheap."

And there was a third factor, one that may have had more to do with blisters than either resin formulations or cost-cutting: a lack of skilled labor. When fiberglass boats appeared in the late 1950s, the work force was wood-trained. This was a mature work force, used to turning out a good-quality product without being rushed. As production increased in the next 20-odd years, younger workers, often not well supervised on the production line, were charged with the critical phase of laminating hulls. Rapid growth in an industry that previously had (and needed) few quality controls due to its small and exclusive nature was in my judgment the leading cause of hull blisters.

Most everyone has seen hull blisters, and most everyone has an opinion on their seriousness. If you subscribe to my view of the principal cause, then you do not want anything to do with a blistered hull, because it indicates that poor laminating procedures caused the problem—and who wants a poorly constructed boat? On the other hand, I have never seen or heard of a boat that sank due to osmotic blistering, and as boats that have this problem sell for less money than those that do not, a repair might be a feasible alternative for a careful buyer. But first a brief explanation of what an osmotic blister is.

When there are minute and not-so-minute voids in the gelcoat on underwater surfaces, and often between the gelcoat and the first layer of tissue or heavier mat beneath it, the hydraulic pressure of the surrounding water pushes moisture through the gelcoat and into those voids. The gelcoat is a semipermeable membrane; it resists but cannot altogether prevent moisture penetration. (Isophthalic polyester resin is more water-resistant than orthophthalic, and its use for gelcoat is increasing as a result.) Once water is in the voids, it interacts with any uncured resins, fiberglass binders, free peroxide catalyst, pigments, and additives, and the result is an acidic, highly concentrated solution. This ion-rich solution induces more moisture to migrate through the gelcoat from the comparatively ion-poor seawater or even more ion-poor fresh water. (Osmosis works more quickly in fresh than in salt water.) That's what osmosis does: By forcing water from the ion-poor to the ion-rich liquid, it attempts to equalize the ionic concentrations of two liquids separated by a semipermeable membrane. Pressure inside the cavities builds up, and ultimately blisters form. When the surveyor punctures one to inspect it, the black acidic goop that is released smells like styrene.

Evaluating the Problem

Some blister problems are worse than others, and how bad they are has a lot to do with the care and skill that went into the laminating process. If a hull has numerous resin-starved dry sections or unbonded voids between layers of the laminate, moisture that breaches the gelcoat barrier can continue to work itself deeper into the succeeding layers, a process called *wicking*. On the other hand, a very tight and well wetted-out laminate behind the gelcoat would stop the process for some time, and would not offer the water as much in the way of chemical compounds with which to create an acidic solution; broken blisters on such a hull would likely release only slightly acidic salt or fresh water.

Blisters very rarely cover the entire underwater surface of the hull. Most cases are confined to small areas or patches, but can spread over time. Let's say the surveyor opens these and finds no acidic solution present. The moisture levels of the hull are at an acceptable level for the age and materials used. Is the surveyor supposed to "flunk" the boat out of hand? I think not, although it makes me nervous to say so. It is at this point that the surveyor and his client need to have a very good understanding of each other. Some buyers cannot accept a flawed product, no matter how good the reasoning may be for repairing it, or how much money can be deducted from the price as a result of the problem. If, on the other hand, the buyer is inclined to repair the problem, then the surveyor must identify the extent of the problem and provide his best estimate of how much time and money will be needed to make a lasting repair.

If, after opening several blisters, the surveyor finds that the damage is clearly into the first layer of mat and perhaps even deeper layers, he may ask permission to do what is called a *laminate profile*, a process done with a grinder. In an affected section, about 6 inches square, first the gelcoat is removed and the moisture content measured and recorded, then each successive layer is ground off and the process repeated until dry readings are reached (if ever). This process allows the surveyor to determine how many layers will need to be removed and replaced with new ones, and it allows him to make a more accurate estimate of the repair cost.

Repairs and Prevention

When a hull is virtually covered with blisters and shows a great deal of moisture content, repairs are often made by a process called *peeling*. A clawlike machine, set to a predetermined depth, peels the affected layers of the laminate off the entire bottom. After the exposed laminate is rinsed with fresh hot water, high-intensity heat lamps are used to dry the hull until the moisture levels are low enough to permit the repair to begin. New laminations are substituted for those removed, generally on a one-to-one basis; it has become a common practice to lay these up with vinylester or epoxy resins because of their greater resistance to water. Finally, new gelcoat—probably isophthalic polyester—is sprayed on, or the hull is faired with surfacing putty and painted.

The cost for this type of repair runs at present about $300 to $350 per foot of length. Peeling has a good record of success, and normally the peeler will warranty the work for 10 years or even life.

Is it possible to cure osmosis by local repair and avoid the cost of peeling? In certain situations, I think it is well worth a try. I have monitored quite a number of boats repaired this way, and they have remained blister-free after five to seven years' use. I think the key to this type of repair is to catch the blisters early in their development when they are very small—even rashlike—and are confined to the surface of the first layer of chopped-strand mat below the gelcoat, rather than being deeply embedded. Another plus would be a still-uniform degree of moisture, as measured by a Sovereign or similar meter, over the blistered and nonblistered sections of the hull. It would be advantageous to use a moisture meter that will read deeply inside the laminate (Protimeter for example) rather than just the exterior. The moisture levels are important because it is more difficult to dry a hull with the gelcoat on than when it's off.

Assuming we can get this desirable combination, an alternative to peeling is to remove the existing blisters, clean the small voids, fill them with epoxy thickened with a sandable thixotropic agent such as microballoons, sand to a fair surface, then coat the entire underwater surface, including the unblistered gelcoat, with some 10 to 12 mils of epoxy applied with a roller or brush. Of course the hull has to be dried to an acceptable level (less than 10% on a Sovereign meter) before the coating is applied. The cost of this type of repair on a 40-foot yacht would be the time for preparation of the hull and the cost of the epoxy coating, which 400 if you do it yourself.

The InterProtect system, manufactured by Interlux, has been developed

A hull-peeling machine is a drastic solution when osmosis is too extensive to repair locally. The hull laminates are peeled to a specified depth (top). Then a spray of CSM and vinylester resin starts the new laminates, with rovings added as necessary. Vinylester resins are used in this process because epoxy does not spray well. After the laminates have been replaced, the bottom is faired smooth, and gelcoat and/or an epoxy barrier coat can be applied with a roller (bottom). This process costs about $350 a foot.

to combat blistering. The company offers the System 2000 for use by boat-owners (applied with brush and roller) and the 3000 for spray application by professionals. The former is generally for less severe cases. Both systems comprise a base coating, followed by buildup coats that give a thickness of 10 to 12 mils when the job is completed. The antifouling paint goes over this epoxy barrier coating. Interlux recommends drying the hull for a period of two weeks to two months before applying the coating. You should monitor the drying with a moisture meter (I strongly recommend a surveyor's assistance with this), but if you don't have access to one, use the following method: Tape a sheet of clear plastic, 1 foot square, over all the sections that were blistered. If after 24 hours no condensation shows, the hull can be coated.

Interprotect can be used on new hulls, old hulls without blisters, or after minor and major blister repairs. It is available from outlets in the United States, Europe, and the United Kingdom. More information is available from Interlux Yacht Finishes, 2270 Morris Ave., P.O. Box 386, Union, NJ 07083.

Here are some true and false concepts and common questions about hull blisters:

> *Hull blisters make the boat structurally unsafe for offshore use.* False. I and others estimate that 80 percent of blisters are a cosmetic problem only.
> *Warmer waters speed up osmosis.* True.
> *Fresh water passes through gelcoat faster than salt water.* True.
> *Epoxy resins give better impermeability to water than vinylester, which is more impermeable than the polyesters.* True.
> *It is necessary to dry a hull before making a blister repair.* True.
> *A blistered hull will reduce the market value and insurance value of a boat.* True.
> *Boats that are in the water six months a year have less chance of blistering than boats that are in the water year-round.* True.
> *Will a peeled-hull repair fully protect my boat from ever having another blister problem?* Probably, but ask me in 15 years.
> *Can I remove the blisters, fill the voids with polyester resin filler (autobody putty, for example), and expect this repair to last?* No.

I am indebted to Jamestown Boat Yard and the Hinckley Company for their generous time and expertise in suggesting ways that owners might combat blistering.

Chapter 4

Surveying the Principal Structures

Hull ⁕ Decks ⁕ Deck Hardware ⁕ Propulsion Gear ⁕ Rudder ⁕ Keel ⁕ Bulkheads ⁕ Steering Gear

Surveys are performed in two stages, the first being the out-of-water inspection, and the second, the in-water, or sea-trial, portion. The latter will be discussed in Chapter 5; the procedures covered in this chapter are best performed with the boat hauled.

Before you commence your inspection, the bottom surfaces, rudder, propeller, and shaft should be clean. I would recommend several tools for this part of the job, including a good light, such as a painter's lamp, and a sharp probe or a jackknife. A paint scraper for removing small sections of the antifouling coatings is also necessary.

As mentioned earlier, I begin a survey with a leisurely walk around the hull and deck to look for obvious flaws. These include grounding damage, stress cracks in the hull, keel problems, rudder problems, and signs of unusual stress on deck (deflection of deck surfaces, cracked ports, and related indicators), as discussed in Chapter 2. During this first look at the boat, a surveyor gets a feel for its general condition and maintenance and notes any hard spots showing on the hull laminate, the alignment of the keel and rudder, pitting or scale corrosion of the shaft and prop, and the condition of the shaft Cutless bearing (the rubber bearing sleeved in the strut in many boats).

Laminate Testing

The two primary laminate tests used today are the percussion test and the moisture test. Both of these are simple enough to perform but difficult to interpret, so the conclusions are best drawn by an experienced surveyor. Percussion tests are done with a phenolic (plastic-headed) hammer, or below the waterline with a peening hammer (6-ounce). The point of this test is to locate previous repairs, glass separations, and voids in the laminates, which are found by listening for hollow or soft returns. A good laminate gives a very sharp return. The wide variety of sounds in any hull, caused by internal tanks, reinforcing stringers, bulkheads, water in the bilge, engine beds, or partially cored sections, would confuse a novice. The surveyor taps the entire hull—topsides and bottom—and makes a note of unusual sounds on a sketch pad. Later, during the interior inspection, he notes what stiffener or piece of gear may have caused that return, or determines that it is, in fact, a delaminated (separated) portion of the lay-up or a void (air pocket between laminations of fiberglass). Percussion will normally ferret out any repairs where filler was used, and with the scraper, these areas can be visually inspected to ascertain the depth and seriousness of the repair.

After completing the percussion test, I use either a Sovereign or a Protimeter moisture testing device to assess the moisture content of the laminates. These meters emit microwaves, then record and calibrate the return signal from the laminate. They are not accurate enough to give exact, absolute percentages of moisture, and should under no circumstances be used in this manner. Rather, readings must be interpreted relative to other readings on the boat in question and relative to the tester's experience of what is normal or acceptable in a boat of that age and construction. The meters unfortunately are often used improperly.

Two meters in wide use by surveyors today. The multimeter (left) facilitates standard tests on wiring grounds, resistance, D.C. and A.C. voltages, alternator output, and battery condition. The moisture meter (right) is a microwave instrument that measures the relative moisture in a fiberglass hull or deck. It is scaled to various hull thicknesses, more moisture being allowable in a thick laminate than in a thin one. It is an instrument that requires a lot of experience to use properly; among other variables, cores read somewhat differently than solid laminates. The one shown here is a Protimeter Aquant.

The author moisture-testing an old Bristol 42-foot motorsailer. When done evenly over the entire hull and deck surfaces, moisture-testing will identify inordinately wet areas in a hull or around fittings on deck. Allowances must be made for the age of a hull, and whether it is used 12 months or seasonally. For best results, all coatings (paint) should be removed before measurements are taken.

Their best use is to confirm what the surveyor already suspects as a problem. If he has located visually or by percussion test a suspicious panel section that shows stress cracking or deflection, experience tells him to expect higher moisture content there. The meter will show the extent to which this moisture exceeds a normal, healthy laminate.

The meter can also be used to evaluate a hull's susceptibility to blistering or as an indicator of the seriousness of existing osmosis. By taking readings over the entire underwater surface, the surveyor ascertains an overall moisture content (see illustration on pages 52–53). The question then becomes, what is excessive and what is normal? The moisture content of a 25-year-old boat, for example, should be greater than that of a 2-year-old boat, and in making a correct evaluation, the surveyor must consider the age and the materials involved (solid laminate, balsa-cored, Airex-cored, etc.).

A normal "healthy" reading on the absolute scale is between 4 and 12 percent. Rarely do readings on the bottom of a boat hauled over the winter show less than 4 percent, and when a boat has been in the water for a season and hauled for three days, the readings are going to be higher—say, 8 to 12 percent. If the meter indicates saturation (readings higher than, say, 25 percent) over the entire hull (or deck, for that matter), it's a pretty good indication that all is not well! In a case such as this, the percussion test would have been very negative as well. There are few surprises in this business. The return sounds from the percussion test would be like tapping rotten fruit—dead, with no resonance.

The difficult calls occur when the moisture content is moderate to high, but not yet near saturation. On the Sovereign meter, this area is in the absolute scale at about 15 to 18 percent. Let's say we have a boat undergoing survey that shows a reading of 15 percent. The percussion tests were acceptable, still good-quality resonance, no unusual stress-induced hull fatigue, evidently good maintenance by the owner. No osmosis is present. At this stage, a surveyor will tell his client that while he does not see anything structurally deficient in the boat, the moisture content is elevated, which could be an indication that the hull will develop osmosis-related problems at some later date. That date is impossible to predict. I have seen hulls showing 18 to 20 percent moisture with nary a blister, and I have seen blisters on boats showing 8 percent. A heavy solid laminate can take more moisture than a thin-skinned balsa-cored construction, due to the potential of wet core and delamination of the skin-to-core bond in the latter.

The shortcoming of the moisture meter has been its inability to record moisture levels below the surface of the laminate. Some newer meters, such as the Protimeter Aquant, purport to read deeper levels. Any meter can be inaccurate, however, if used on a boat that has just been hauled for survey. The boat should not be moisture-tested until 36 hours have passed, giving the surface time to dry. Hulls will read considerably dryer after just two hours out of the water.

Rudders and skegs also are tested by percussion and moisture meter, although finding high levels of moisture in foam-cored rudders is nearly an everyday proposition. As discussed earlier, the lower third of the spade rudder is now made to tear away if it sustains a hard enough hit. So, we examine the fairness (smoothness) of the blade surface to note if moisture has been active enough to cause any swelling that would separate the halves of the blade. Normally a rudder with fair surfaces and clean joint lines that is well secured around the rudderpost entry is going to be all right. Tapping rudders involves differentiating between the foam-cored sections and the rigid steel reinforcements inside the blade. A solid-laminate rudder is inspected in the same manner, but its resonance is more apt to be like that of a hull. The weak point of all rudders is the join line of the two halves, and it is not unusual to find splits and water leaking from these, especially after a cold winter when moisture has frozen inside and expanded the blade surfaces.

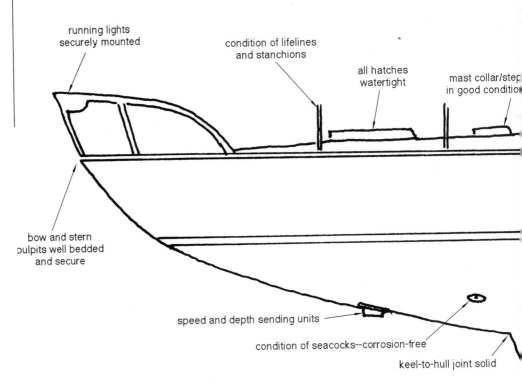

running lights
securely mounted

condition of lifelines
and stanchions

all hatches
watertight

mast collar/step
in good condition

bow and stern
pulpits well bedded
and secure

speed and depth sending units

condition of seacocks--corrosion-free

keel-to-hull joint solid

condition o

Some key items for inspection on the exterior hull and decks. (For indicators of the condition of the hull and deck laminates themselves, see Chapter 2.)

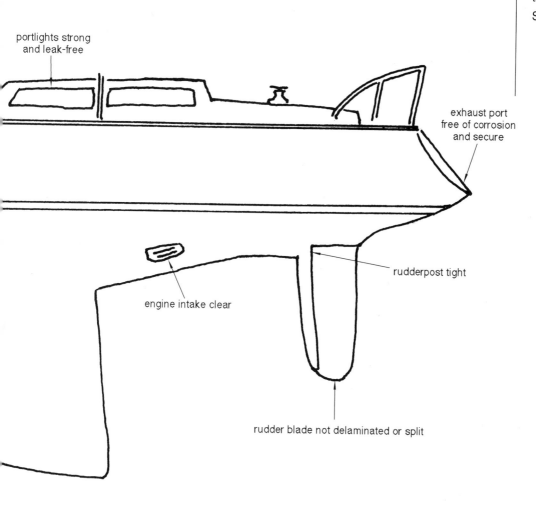

portlights strong
and leak-free

exhaust port
free of corrosion
and secure

rudderpost tight

engine intake clear

rudder blade not delaminated or split

53

Seacocks and Hoses

An average-size cruising boat may have anywhere from 4 to 10 inlet and discharge valves, commonly called *seacocks*. Because they are below the waterline, they are extremely important in a survey report. One failure will sink your boat. Valves are of two types, the *gate valve* and the *ball valve*; the latter is considered more reliable, especially for offshore use.

Seacocks are traditionally bronze castings, which, if made in the U.S., are generally very good. If made in Taiwan, watch out! There is now a trend toward seacocks and through hulls made of plastics such as Delrin and Marelon; these can be perfectly acceptable on small vessels—say, under 30 feet. Whatever the material, an indication of testing and approval by the Underwriters' Laboratory is a good idea. The first part of a valve and associated through-hull inspection is the exterior one, in which the coating of antifouling or fairing material is removed so that the exterior flange of the through-hull can be inspected. What we are looking for in a bronze through hull is hairline cracks, corrosion deterioration, pitting and scaling, and a green or pink tinge. Green could indicate some electrochemical reaction; pink might indicate a loss of zinc in the casting, causing embrittlement. A sharp rap with a peening hammer on the flange should indicate whether it is brittle enough to crack. The old-style flanges protrude from the hull, and the surveyor by inserting a knife blade can

A typical ¾-inch bronze ball-valve seacock, found, for example, on a water-closet inlet, an engine seawater inlet, a saltwater pump inlet, a sink drain, cockpit scuppers, etc. I often find these without handles, and can't figure out how they get closed in an emergency. The round barrel, or body, is removable for greasing. The flange on the bottom is bolted through a backing plate inside the hull. Bronze seacocks must be inspected for corrosion, either electromechanical or galvanic (dissimilar metal reactions), cracks, leaks, and ease of operation. The hoses and clamps leading from them are just as important!

(Right) *Exploded view of a ball-valve seacock.* (Jim Sollers illustration from *Boatowner's Mechanical and Electrical Manual,* by Nigel Calder, International Marine, 1990)

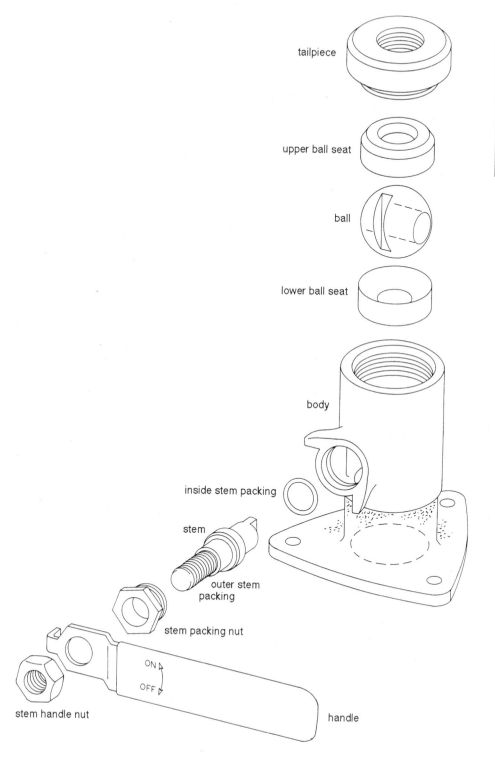

tailpiece

upper ball seat

ball

lower ball seat

body

inside stem packing

stem

outer stem
packing

stem packing nut

ON
OFF

stem handle nut

handle

see how much tolerance there is between the hull and the flange base and if the bedding material has begun to wear away. When this bedding fails, the laminate around the flange, unprotected by gelcoat, slowly absorbs water. This can cause a local softening of the laminate. To check for this, apply pressure with the head of a hammer on the area some two inches surrounding the seacock to see if it will flex under a load. Use a probe judiciously as well. If you note the bedding is poor, or there is any weeping inside the vessel at the valve itself, then remove the through hull, inspect the laminate, and if all is well, rebed the through hull. This is a serious matter, and I recommend that any boat 10 years old have all the sea-

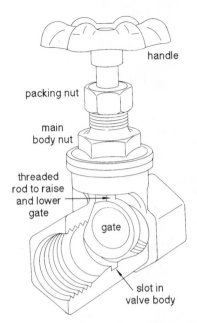

Anatomy of a gate valve. (Jim Sollers illustration from *Boatowner's Mechanical and Electrical Manual*, by Nigel Calder, International Marine, 1990)

(Above and right) *The trouble with gate valves. Both these bronze valves, mounted on cockpit scupper outlets, were frozen open. Twisting the handle is supposed to turn a threaded rod inside the gate, thus forcing it down to seal off the passageway, but all efforts with heat, penetrating oil, and various "persuaders" failed to break the corrosion bonding of the rod to the gate. Finally* (right) *one of the rods simply sheared off. Fortunately the boat was out of the water at the time.* (Photos courtesy Jonathan Eaton)

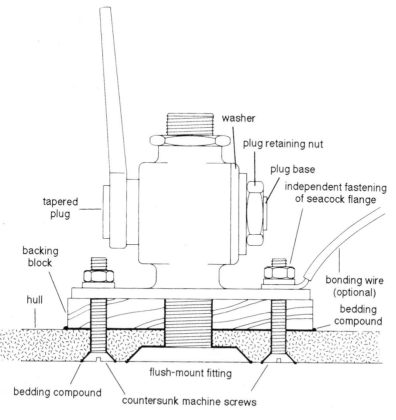

washer

plug retaining nut

plug base

independent fastening
of seacock flange

tapered
plug

backing
block

bonding wire
(optional)

hull

bedding
compound

flush-mount fitting

bedding compound

countersunk machine screws

Proper seacock installation requires a good, thick backing block, molded as necessary on its exterior face to conform to the hull contour. The through-hull neck and flange pieces must be well bedded. (from Marine Diesel Engines, *by Nigel Calder, International Marine, 1991)*

cocks and through hulls pulled, inspected, and rebedded or replaced. A similar inspection is made on the inside of the boat, with good light and a magnifying glass to help you spot hairline cracks in the castings.

Whether gate or ball type, the valve has to work. If a hose fails, you have to be able to close it. Good ball valves can be removed and serviced with waterproof grease, a good idea every year or two, and they should give years of good service. Gate valves, on the other hand, combine too many metals to remain problem-free over the long haul. The casting and gate are bronze, the valve stem is stainless, and the handles are steel. These just deteriorate and fall off into the bilge. If you must have gate valves, get stainless handles too!

Hoses connected to sea valves should not be clear plastic or garden variety. You need high-quality, thick-walled flexible hose, double-clamped at the valve connection. Existing hose showing stiffness, cracking, checking, or collapsing should be replaced promptly. Many yachtsmen tie a tapered softwood plug, appropriately sized to plug the seacock opening, to all valves for emergency purposes.

Propeller Shafts and Bearings

Auxiliary sailboats most often use marine-grade stainless steel or bronze for propeller shafts. Monel and Aquamet are far superior in strength, but are usually considered too expensive for stock boats. Shafts need to be true (straight) and free of corrosion. The visual inspection should note any wasting or pitting from galvanic or electrolytic corrosion. Inspect the shaft coupling bolts for any signs of looseness. Usually the shaft is prevented from slipping in the coupling by a key, and prevented from backing out by one or two set screws. These must be wired closed. No one likes losing their propeller shaft out of the boat when backing down! Inspect the shaft bearing for any wear or slack, the key pin that prevents slippage of the prop around the shaft, the two nuts that secure the prop, and the cotter pin on the shaft tail. Sailboats wear out Cutless (shaft) bearings about every three to four years on average, and this can be accelerated by the use of folding propellers. The condition of a bearing can be judged by firmly grasping the end of the shaft and applying pressure vertically, then laterally. Little more than $\frac{1}{8}$ inch of play is acceptable, and none is preferable. Check the rubber in a water-lubricated bearing for signs of cracking, and inspect the snugness of the set screws that hold the bearing secure in the strut. Full-keel yachts with attached rudders do not have a strut bearing (P-bracket). Rather, the bearing is lagged or bolted at the end of the

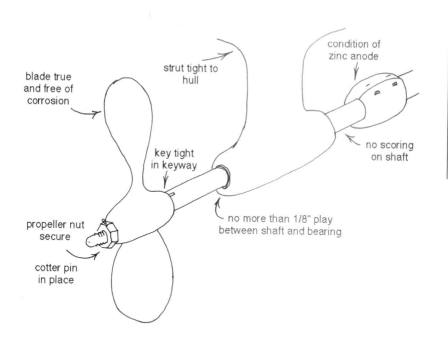

*Inspection of the propeller shaft, strut, and Cutless bearing. There should be a
locknut (not shown here) snugged up against the propeller nut.*

shaft log, but the basic inspection is
the same.

Shaft alignment is an important
consideration for the surveyor. Align-
ments are better evaluated in the
water than out (see Chapter 5), but
if you cannot have a sea trial, as in a
winter inspection, then a close visual
inspection of the shaft while rotating
(dialing) the propeller, perhaps with

*A badly corroded (scale corrosion)
propeller, with nicked blade tips, on a
full-keel design with attached rudder.
The proximity of the flat rudder edge to
this prop could cause a considerable
problem with prop wash. The numbers
in chalk are moisture readings.*

the aid of a jig, will allow you to note any extreme irregularities.

Rudderposts

We have discussed the inherent weaknesses of the foam-cored spade rudder, but another consideration—unless the boat under survey has an outboard rudder—is the amount of play between the rudderpost and the tube that supports it inside the boat. There are three schools of rudder installation these days. The "cheap" school just runs the post into a tube without any bearings, and may force some lubrication into the tube via a grease fitting. The next step up is to insert nylon, Teflon, or Delrin bushings (perhaps an upper and a lower) inside the tube. The third method uses ball bearings in the tube. A tube with bushings or bearings is better performing and more durable over the long run. Plastic bushings are a lot less expensive than ball bearings and fairly easy to replace. In any event, when too much play is present, the rudderpost will either rattle in the tube when the boat is underway, or it will

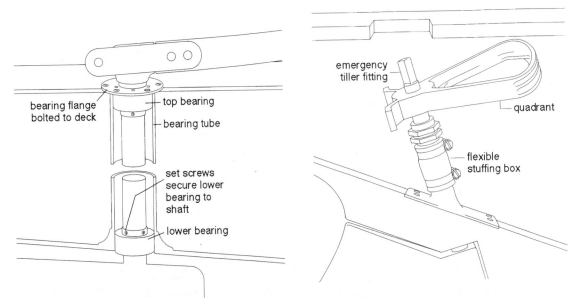

bearing flange
bolted to deck

top bearing

bearing tube

set screws
secure lower
bearing to
shaft

lower bearing

emergency
tiller fitting

quadrant

flexible
stuffing box

A well-constructed rudderpost configuration for tiller steering with a top bearing (left), and a typical arrangement for wheel steering without a top bearing (right). (Jim Sollers illustration from Boatowner's Mechanical and Electrical Manual, by Nigel Calder, International Marine, 1990) develop friction and make steering more difficult. Movement of the post also puts additional stress on the steering cables of a wheel-steered boat, and can chafe or stretch them, causing slack steering.

By grasping the lower section of the blade and forcing it fore and aft and then laterally, the surveyor can tell how much play is in the shaft. With tiller steering more play can be tolerated, because it won't induce collateral wear on an attached cable-and-quadrant system, but the slap and wobble will still be present and annoying, if nothing else. What is a tolerable amount of play? It really depends on the resulting symptoms underway, and boats differ, but as a yardstick I would say that less than ¼ inch is ideal. More than 1 inch indicates the need to add grease to the tube, replace a fitted plastic bushing in the tube, or replace or install actual bearings in the tube.

Rubbing Strakes and Toerails

A wooden rubbing strake mounted on the topsides below the sheer, also known as a rubrail and seen mostly on larger, heavier, older designs, is designed to absorb impact stresses from a variety of angles and should therefore have some interior backing or reinforcement. This can be a partial core in the topsides or more properly a piece of hardwood on the inside of the hull to which the strake is through-bolted. It would be desirable to have this piece of wood glassed to the inside of the hull. Although through-bolting is best, threaded screw fastenings are common when rubrails are mounted on smaller craft.

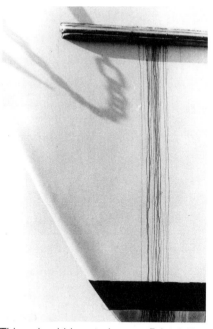

The toerail or caprail covers the hull-to-deck joint on most sailing vessels. As such it has to be as watertight a covering as possible, and this depends on the closeness of the fit

This oak rubbing strake on a Bristol 42 was not bedded well, and the fastenings have deteriorated. Water got behind the oak and rotted it, and the result is the "bleeding" on the hull. In this case, the entire rail had to be replaced.

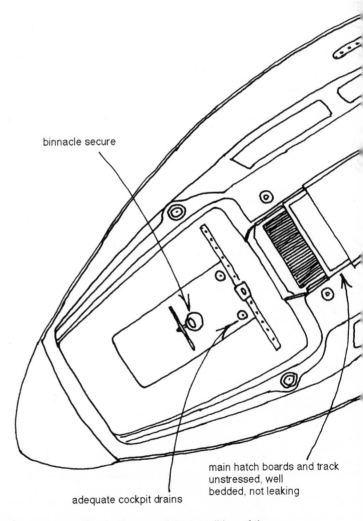

binnacle secure

main hatch boards and track
unstressed, well
bedded, not leaking

adequate cockpit drains

*Some key items for inspection on deck. (For indicators of the condition of the
deck laminates themselves, see Chapter 2.)*

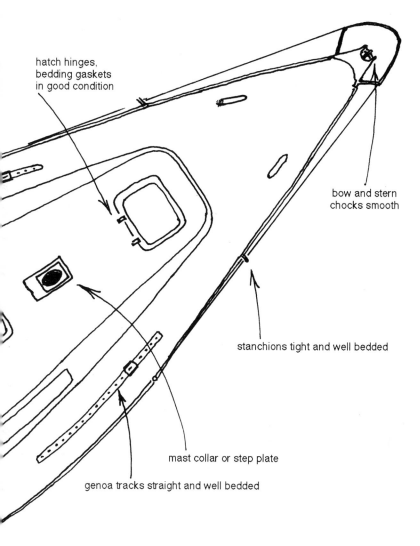

hatch hinges,
bedding gaskets
in good condition

bow and stern
chocks smooth

stanchions tight and well bedded

mast collar or step plate

genoa tracks straight and well bedded

and the type of bedding, or sealant, used. Normally the surveyor can ascertain the type and condition of the sealant by going inside the vessel and inspecting the exposed underside of the joint, checking for hardening or shrinking of the sealant and signs of leakage. Few things are more frustrating than hull-deck joints hidden by an interior fiberglass liner. Unfortunately, the boats in which this occurs tend also to be the boats in which the deck is fastened with self-tapping screws or pop rivets rather than through-bolts and is therefore more at risk of leaking or coming adrift.

Teak toerails almost always need to be removed after 12 to 15 years, cleaned, and rebedded. This is something an owner, with a friend belowdecks, can do by removing the bungs on the toerails and accessing the machine screw heads. The inside person holds the nuts in place while the outside person backs out the bolts. Then the rail is gingerly pried loose, and all components are thoroughly cleaned and resurfaced before the new bedding is applied. I would recommend a polysulfide adhesive sealant, because it will remain flexible and the rail can be removed years later, if necessary, without dynamite.

Rails, Stanchions, and Deck Hardware

In Chapter 2, we discussed the weaknesses of rails and stanchions and the reinforcements they need. When inspecting a boat, one must also observe whether the rails, stanchions, and other deck hardware—lifelines, ports and hatches, cleats, etc.—are suitable for their intended use. By suitable I mean, are they strong enough? For offshore use, all the deck hardware needs to be well reinforced with strong backing plates under the deck; there should be enough stanchions, not just a token two or three per side; and the lifelines should be doubles made of heavy stranded wire. Portlights should be relatively small, and elliptical if possible, to prevent them from being breached by heavy breaking seas, and opening ports should have high-quality bronze or stainless steel (not plastic) frames with strong dogs (latches). Lexan-type hatches ought to be reinforced with a grid under the plastic, and so on. A conscientious surveyor looking at an offshore boat will examine the size of the cockpit scuppers, which should be large enough to drain the cockpit quickly if a wave poops the boat. (Depending of course on the volume of the cockpit, this usually means a diameter of at least 1¼ inches, and often 2 inches or more on big boats.) He'll check the ability to securely dog the anchor locker if access is via a deck hatch (this is always too lightly done in production craft), and in general the ability to dog hatches both from the deck and the interior of the vessel.

Structural Bulkheads and Stiffeners

We move now to a visual inspection of the interior structures, beginning with the stiffeners molded into the hull to support the wide expanses of fiberglass. These include fore-and-aft stiffeners, or longitudinals; athwartships stiffeners; and the floors, which help support the ballast of an external keel. Without stiffeners, the hull would twist or flex, which degrades performance and ultimately destroys the structure.

Stiffeners are fabricated into the hull during the lay-up and are generally preformed and either hollow or foam-cored. They should be inspected for cracking or separation from the fiberglass layers securing them, either of which would indicate the presence of stress. The number of stringers used in a hull has a lot to do with the quality of the build. In order to examine the stiffeners, the surveyor has to take up the interior cabin sole and berth covers. If a full pan liner is fitted, he'll have to shine a good light up under the bilge access boards to either side, possibly using a mirror to extend the field of view. Chapter 2 discussed the frequent inadequacy of stiffeners in the bow and quarter sections of boats, especially smaller sailboats, and the possible consequences.

The last structural members to be inspected are the bulkheads. In a standard traditional layout there are five sets, the forwardmost of which is the chain locker bulkhead. Next aft is the bulkhead at the after end of the forward cabin and then the *main bulkhead* at the forward end of the main cabin. These two often demarcate the water closet, or head, and the hanging lockers. Then there are the half or partial bulkheads to port and starboard at the after end of the main cabin that form the galley and nav-station partitions, and last the sail locker and/or the lazarette bulkhead. In modern designs without a transom overhang, the lazarette bulkhead has all but disappeared.

I think a good bulkhead installation ought to have the following characteristics: First, it should be bonded to the hull and decks continuously around its perimeter, rather than just in selected locations on the sides and bottom. Second, there needs to be a cushion between the sharp edge of the bulkhead and the hull shell; otherwise, a hard spot may develop and crack the exterior gelcoat. These cushions can be in the form of foam strips, or wood fillets that increase the width of the edge, or both. Third, as the bulkheads are generally secured in place by fiberglass tape laid up with polyester resin, the bond to the wood surface has to be good, and it should be fairly wide—I think about 4 to 5 inches on a 35- to 40-foot vessel. (Two to 3 inches is fairly typical on a 30-footer.) It should comprise several layers of fiberglass, each one a little wider than the one beneath so as to maintain some direct contact with the bulkhead and hull shell. Good builders etch or score the bulkhead surface for better adhesion of the tape, and in the best construction the bond to the wooden bulkhead is reinforced with mechanical fasteners. Some European builders through-bolt the tabs and the bulkheads, which I think is a good practice.

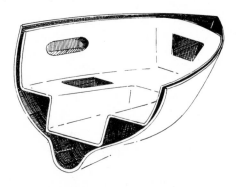

Solid fiberglass hull liner showing limited accessibility of the hull for repair. Sometimes the liner is made up of subassemblies, particularly in the head area; these can ease access. The headliner is almost always a separate molding. (from *Fiberglass Boat Repair Manual,* by Allan Vaitses, International Marine, 1988)

One of the recurring problems I find with bulkheads on racing boats stems from their flat, shallow bilges, where water is in constant contact with the bulkhead tabbing. If the tabbing loosens (which it's likely to do as the wood alternately swells and shrinks in moist/dry cycles), the water collects in the void and eventually begins to rot the bottom of the bulkhead. What starts as a cosmetic problem soon enough becomes a structural one. Through-bolted angle brackets are particularly helpful for tabbings in the bilge area.

Some manufacturers would have you believe that a full interior liner is going to provide all the support that would otherwise be provided by stringers and bulkheads. Too often, however, the liners are nothing more than cosmetic, covering an unreinforced hull shell. When you see a liner that is badly cracked or twisted, it is generally an indication of this problem.

When bulkhead problems exist, they are fairly easily detected. For one thing, doors begin to jam when their bulkheads shift. When tabbing breaks and bulkheads come adrift, any movement or separation can generally be plainly seen. Unfairness of the large surface of the bulkhead might indicate pressure being exerted, or you will see hard spots from the bulkheads on the exterior inspection of the hull. It is a good idea to use an awl or knife blade judiciously at the corners of all the tabbing connections, but especially at the bottom edge where it comes into contact with water. Check for soft wood. And incidentally, loose bulkheads can be retabbed or, if the existing tabbings are adrift but still intact, mechanically refastened with new adhesive sealant. The size of the job depends in part on accessibility, but it can be done.

The Hull-Keel Join

Now we come to the join of the keel ballast to the hull on an externally ballasted vessel. I have said my preference is for a heavy fiberglass stubby molded into the hull, through which the keel can be bolted, but some boats have deep, high-aspect keels bolted to a much smaller stubby or flush to the molded hull bottom. Now you have this large vertical surface with high lateral plane, and only a relatively small surface to bolt to, and it's going to generate plenty of stress even without being subjected to a grounding. There are two principal methods of attaching keels mechanically. One is to place the keel bolts in line, and generally make them pretty hefty, say 1- to ¼-inch diameter, and the other is to place them side by side in pairs using slightly smaller-diameter bolts, say ½ to ¾ inch.

In order to further strengthen the keel-to-hull join, it is common to install bilge floors, very similar to those in a wooden boat, and to take the bolts up through the floors before attaching the nuts. This has the effect of distributing the ballast load over a greater surface area. This is a critical inspection area, and the surveyor needs to take good care in evaluating the strength along the centerline. Any and all stress damage there must be remedied, including cracks in the stubby, broken or cracked floors, loose or broken floor-to-hull tabbing, elongation of keelbolt holes resulting in leaks through them, and any serious corrosion on the bolts themselves. Quite often I find plain steel washers placed under the stainless steel nuts in the bilge, and after some years these deteriorate and slack develops. This causes a separation of the join between the lead and the stubby or hull, leading to increased torsional stress and leaking.

Steering Gear

Edson International, of New Bedford, Massachusetts, has long had the corner on steering gear used in wheel-steered sailboats. The predominant gear is the cable, or pedestal, type, in which the wheel turns a sprocket, which in turn drives a chain inside the binnacle leading to 7 x 19 stainless wire. (The

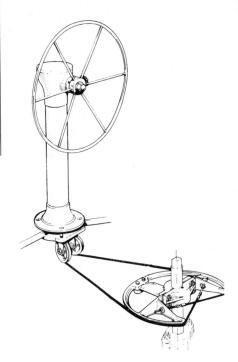

Cable steering is the most common type by far. Shown here are open-cable steering using a radial, or disc, drive at the rudderpost, and open-cable steering using a quadrant. (from *Boatowner's Mechanical and Electrical Manual,* by Nigel Calder, International Marine, 1990)

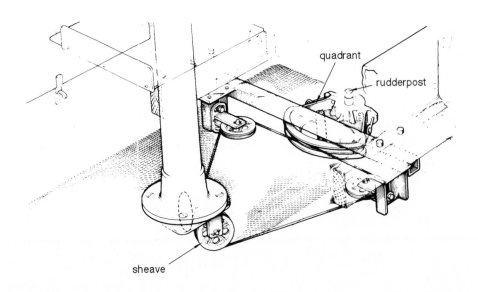

quadrant

rudderpost

sheave

A commonly used cast bronze steering quadrant. The cables below are led from fairleading sheaves, around the face of the quadrant, and aft to the eyebolt deadends, where adjustment for slack can be made. The overhead beam supports the rudderpost from wiggle, and the post protrudes to allow an emergency tiller to be affixed if the gear fails. Just visible below the quadrant is the rudderpost packing gland. Both the steering gear and the packing gland are among the most neglected items on a sailing craft. The wire must be tensioned, greased, and free of breaks; the fairleads should be neat and solid; and the packing gland, if below the waterline, will add a lot of unwanted water to the bilge if not kept packed and adjusted.

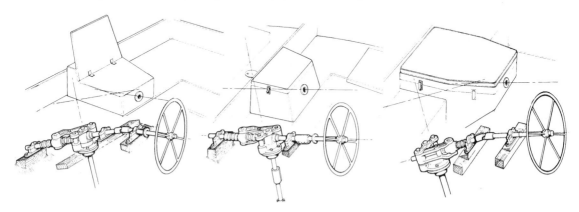

Three configurations of a worm-drive pedestal steering mechanism. The unit can be adapted to a variety of boats by the use of U-joints. Should the worm seize in operation, the steerer can be unbolted from the rudderhead and the emergency tiller substituted. (from Boatowner's Mechanical and Electrical Manual, by Nigel Calder, International Marine, 1990)

1 x 19 construction is not flexible enough for steering cable.) The wire then runs through fairleads to sheaves located in a baseplate (called the *idler plate*) at the bottom of the pedestal, and from there aft to the rudderpost, where the two ends are secured either to a circular fitting *(radial-drive steering)* or a quadrant. Cockpit construction, space, accessibility, and spatial relationships govern the details of the installation (number and location of turning sheaves, quadrant versus radial drive, etc.). Radial systems work very well when the disc is roughly level with the binnacle baseplate and the rudderpost is close to vertical. When the rudderpost is angled, or the heights are unequal, a quadrant system must be used, with an extra set of fairleading sheaves to lead the wire at a proper angle into the quadrant. Quadrant systems always require outboard turning sheaves between the baseplate and the rudderpost.

Rack-and-pinion pedestal-drive steering.
(Courtesy Edson International)

When it is desirable to get the binnacle out of the cockpit to open up more space, or for control of a very large rudder that would stress the components of a cable-driven system, a worm gear or a rack-and-pinion system can be used instead. Neither requires the use of wire, and both are sturdy. Proper alignment of the worm gear is critical to its long-term wear and reliability; the rack and pinion is just about foolproof, but I think both these systems (and particularly the worm gear) are poor in terms of helm feel. They are most often seen on heavy-displacement sailboats (traditional schooners, for example).

Steering-gear failures account for a large percentage of accidents in sailboats, and not a few very hairy moments when the gear lets go suddenly! I think this is caused by the fact that steering compartments are often difficult to access, and the systems are not well understood. As a result, they get little or no maintenance but require adjustments at the very least every year, and sometimes a second time during the season as the wire stretches.

Determine what type of system you have. (I'll bet more than 95 percent of wheel steerers are cable-driven.) Next—and this is also relevant to a tiller-steered boat with an inboard rudder—determine if the system uses a packing gland (stuffing box) on the ruddertube inside the hull. (Unless the fiberglass ruddertube extends so high above the waterline as to render a stuffing box unnecessary, you will find one.) If so, inspect the hoses, clamps, and casting for wear, corrosion, cracks, and leaks, and plan to replace anything that is in questionable condition. If the fitting is leaking, back off the locknut, then tighten the packing nut while holding the shaft with a wrench so that it can't turn. When the flow stops, snug up the locknut. If you cannot stop the flow of water, then the flax packing has worn away and will have to be replaced. This is more easily done out of the water, and for the most part is necessary only on older designs. Newer designs tend to have their rudders hung farther aft than the older full-keel, counter-stern boats, and their ruddertubes extend well above the waterline, so they rarely need packing glands.

The mechanically fastened parts of the cable-driven steering gear are as follows: The quadrant or radial disc is bolted to the rudderpost and should have self-locking nuts if possible—you don't want these to loosen and come off. There has to be a locking collar around the rudderpost, normally under the quadrant, which prevents the rudderpost from slipping lower and binding the quadrant. Make sure this is securely in place. Sometimes the locking collar is installed on deck.

Systems in which the post is inside a fiberglass tube may have a grease fitting. Make sure this is kept full and turned down every month or so during the season.

The steering cable attaches to the quadrant or disc via two eyebolts, which are threaded so that the system can be adjusted for slack. Inspect the wire for burrs or breaks. None are acceptable. If it's slack, tension the wire at the eyebolts. About an inch of deflection along the horizontal runs of the wire should be adequate. If it's too tight, the wire will chafe on the sheaves.

Keep the entire unit clean and well greased. Once in a while the binnacle should be opened (compass removed) and the sprocket greased. At the same time you might get to lubricate the throttle and shift brackets if they are so mounted.

As for the worm-gear and rack-and-pinion systems, these fail mostly in the universal joints, the pinion teeth, or wear on the worm gears. There are quite a few mechanical fastenings on the systems—mainly machine bolts, nuts, and sometimes lags that require normal maintenance and lots of grease.

Chapter 5

Surveying the Mechanical and Electrical Systems

Engines ❋ Generators ❋ Pumps and Motors ❋ Charging Systems

Having evaluated a boat's hull, decks, and principal structures, we turn now to the mechanical/electrical portion of the survey, including engine, generators, charging and electrical systems, and pumps and motors. In the next chapter we'll look at the rig.

There is little consistency of approach among surveyors when it comes to mechanical systems. One surveyor is competent with machinery, while the next may not "do" engines at all! In the latter case the prospective buyer has to pay about the same amount for the hull survey, then spend almost as much again to have the engine evaluated. Clearly you get a better value when you hire a surveyor who can provide both services.

One of the pleasures of surveying machinery, as opposed to hulls, is that there are fewer gray areas. A machine either works or it doesn't, and one is not constantly faced with determining what is normal wear and tear versus actual damage, as is necessary with a hull. Machinery is almost always a high priority in a boat purchase-and-sale agreement, so that any problems found are either repaired prior to the sale or occasion further negotiations between seller and prospective buyer.

Engines

The average survey, let us say on a 40-foot boat, requires four to seven hours for hull, rig, and machinery. Although a surveyor can't dismantle an engine, transmission, and cooling system in this time, he can and should evaluate the "fixed" equipment. This includes the condition of the engine beds and mounts, the shaft coupling, the stuffing box, all hoses and clamps, and wiring connections. This should be followed by an inspection of the oil pan, freeze plugs, engine and transmission (gearbox) seals (for leaks), blistered paint that might indicate overheating, integrity of the fuel lines and their connections at

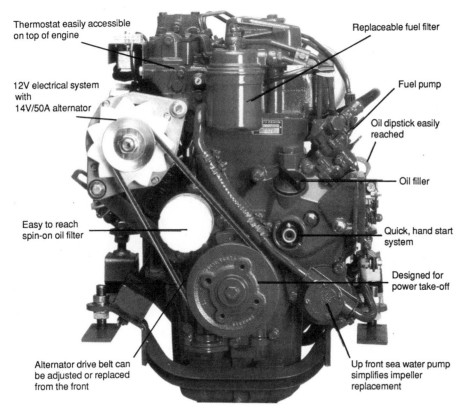

Thermostat easily accessible on top of engine

Replaceable fuel filter

12V electrical system with 14V/50A alternator

Fuel pump

Oil dipstick easily reached

Easy to reach spin-on oil filter

Oil filler

Quick, hand start system

Designed for power take-off

Alternator drive belt can be adjusted or replaced from the front

Up front sea water pump simplifies impeller replacement

The surveyor's most frequent view of an engine. General access can be ascertained—good, bad, or average. The condition of the engine mounts and beds, hoses and clamps, belts and tension, and alternator bracket should be determined. The raw-water pump can be inspected and leaks in the cooling or fuel delivery systems can be detected during the sea trials. (from *Marine Diesel Engines*, by Nigel Calder, International Marine, 1991) the lift pumps and injector nozzles, tension and wear of the pulley belts, the seawater pump's impeller, the clutch and throttle control cables, and brackets.

A conscientious surveyor will note the overall paint detailing of the engine block and gearbox. He also will evaluate the accessibility of important maintenance areas. For instance, if a water heater has been installed so that it blocks access to the stuffing box except by jackhammer, that fact should appear on the surveyor's report.

Other visual inspections, such as the sump oil and transmission fluid on the dipsticks, can indicate trouble in progress. Water in the sump oil leaves bubble traces on the stick and can give the engine oil a brownish tinge. Gear fluids get milky with seawater.

The majority of sailboat auxiliaries are freshwater-cooled diesels of 20 to 85 h.p., two to six cylinders. It is generally speaking true that most of the problems these engines experience relate to fuel or cooling. The cooling systems rely on two pumps—an external centrifugal-type for circulating seawater through the heat exchanger, and the belt-driven water pump attached to the engine to circulate fresh water through the engine's water jacket. The cool seawater absorbs the heat from the engine's coolant, which is similar to the coolant in an automobile engine. In order for the complete cooling system to work properly, the seawater pump has to be in good repair, and the heat exchanger core has to be free of blockage. Restrictions in the core or a badly worn impeller in the pump will cause the engine to overheat. Slight increases in normal operating temperatures can indicate this condition. To restrict corrosion buildup on the seawater side of a heat exchanger, a small pencil zinc anode is fitted inside the unit. This has to be changed, depending on salinity, at least once a year.

Overheating often shows up as a hot spot on the heat exchanger, where the paint is blistering or lifting. I recommend to relatively inexperienced buyers of used boats that they have the heat exchangers cleaned before they take delivery of the boat, and then repeat the cleaning once every three years as normal maintenance.

(Right) *Exploded view of a saltwater pump, which supplies the engine cooling system or the heat exchangers of a freshwater system. Abnormally high temperatures or a loss or lessening of the exhaust water flow could indicate a problem here. 1. Cover. 2. Gasket. 3. Impeller (splined type). 4. Wear plate. 5. Cover retaining screws. 6. Cam (mounted inside the body of the pump). 7. Cam's retaining screw. 8. Pump body. 9. Slinger (to deflect leaks away from the bearing). 10. Bearing. 11. Bearing's retaining circlip. 12. Shaft retaining circlip. 13. Outer seal. 14–16. Inner seal assembly, lip type. 17. (alternative) Inner seal assembly, carbon-ceramic type. 18. Pump shaft. 19. Drive key. (Courtesy ITT/JABSCO)*

A good engine installation offers complete access from either side and the top. In an aft-cabin motorsailer this is usually available. Too often, however, in gaining greater interior space, the engine room access (and ventilation) is sacrificed, with literally no access to the stuffing box, drive belts, or starters.

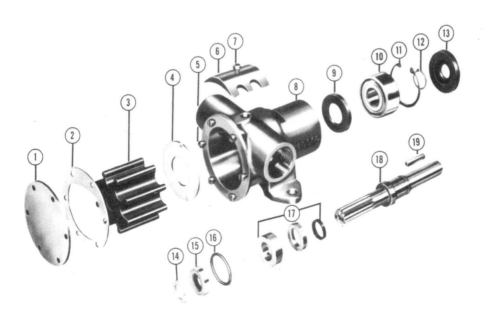

Inside view of a freshwater circulating pump for the closed system on a freshwater-cooled engine. It is one of the more suspicious ingredients of a chronic overheating problem, when all other avenues have been explored. Too much tension on a drive belt can ruin the seals and cause these to fail.

The exhaust manifold "riser" comes off the block and leads to the muffler. It is generally sloped downward to prevent backfilling the engine with seawater. A common area of deterioration on older engines, it must not leak.

Traces of oil in the engine cool-ant—found on the expansion tank cap or in samples of coolant from the tank (the radiator)—could indicate a failed head gasket or even internal block corrosion causing a breach in the water jacket.

The transmission oil cooler, found most often on larger diesel engines (60 h.p. and up), is similar to the engine's heat exchanger. Transmission oil circulates through the core of the cooler and gives up heat to the water surrounding the tubing. If an oil cooler fails, most

This marine oil cooler for transmission fluid operates on the same principle as the engine heat exchanger. If the cores get clogged, the cooling declines or ceases, and you can burn out the gearbox or fill it with salt water. This is one reason why the zinc anodes on the saltwater side must be opened up for inspection and changed periodically.

often because of pinholes in the cooling tubes, oil and salt water mix, and the gears will eventually fail from lack of adequate lubrication. As mentioned,

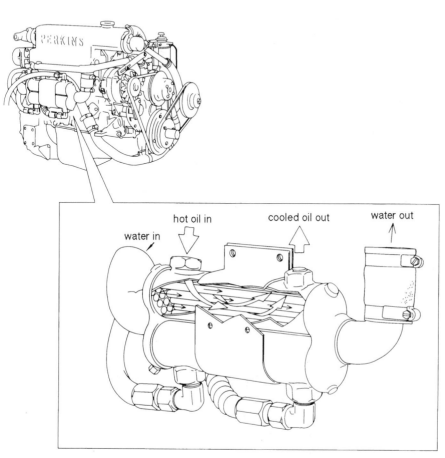

A Perkins multicooler unit, which on this engine cools both the engine oil and the gear oil. On some engines these functions are served by two coolers. Pinholes in the tubing allow the hot oil to mingle with the cooling water, and this will ultimately cause the engine or gear to fail. Milky fluids indicate the presence of salt water. (Jim Sollers illustration, from *Marine Diesel Engines,* by Nigel Calder, International Marine, 1991)

gear oils will turn milky when they mix with salt water, and you can see this on the dipstick. The oil cooler requires the same servicing as the engine's heat exchanger, usually including the zinc. (Some coolers don't have a zinc.)

anode

Internal-block zinc anode on a saltwater-cooled Yanmar diesel engine. These anodes help retard corrosion in the cooling water passages and are changed once or twice per year depending on the salinity of the waters. (from *Marine Diesel Engines,* by Nigel Calder, International Marine, 1991)

Sea Trials and Load Tests

In areas that have cold winters, boats are laid up for six months or more, and engine surveys often have to be done when the boat is out of the water. While I have not had a particularly bad experience surveying engines this way, I'd rather have the boat in commission so that the engines can be tested under load.

Since the surveyor is not a mechanic in the truest sense of the word, his job is to note what I call overt problems. A sea trial allows the surveyor to observe engines and generators under full operating temperatures and outputs. Engines—gas or diesel—have designed operating speeds (measured in revolutions per minute or r.p.m.), and the surveyor gets the opportunity to run the engine through its full range. This allows him to evaluate its performance and ascertain if it will comfortably reach its peak r.p.m. Sometimes a faulty fuel pump will provide adequate fuel at lower engine speeds but prove inad-

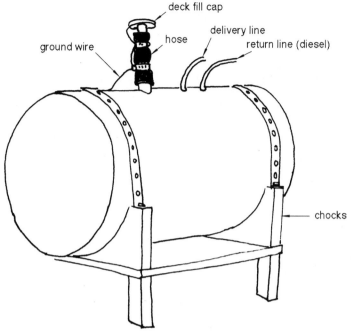

deck fill cap

delivery line

return line (diesel)

hose

ground wire

chocks

Typical fuel-tank installation. Welds, hose, and clamps should be in good condition. Internal baffles want to be welded in place. Tap the tank to seek out weak areas, and look for leaks. Check also for adequate chocking, secure straps, a secure deckplate, and a good connection in the ground wire from the fill pipe to the tank, and then to the engine or the boat's common ground point.

equate as the revs climb, which causes engine performance to break down. The engine manufacturer lists recommended operating temperatures, which will be about 170 to 180 degrees Fahrenheit (77 to 82 degrees Centigrade) for freshwater-cooled engines, and slightly less for seawater-cooled (also known as raw-water-cooled) engines. A good 30 minutes of running time allows for a more accurate assessment of the cooling system and the oil pressure. The latter may fluctuate quite a bit between a cold engine and a warm one, as much as 30 pounds per square inch (psi), and you need to know the pressure at normal operating temperature in order to compare it with the manufacturer's recommended figures.

Water-pump bearings that are near failure don't act up until they get hot and begin to make noise. The same is so for the other pulley-driven systems—saltwater pumps and alternator bearings. The surveyor gets a chance to see and hear all of these symptoms firsthand during a sea trial.

Small sailboat diesels in the 8- to 15-horsepower range tend to have one or two cylinders, and they vibrate more than three-, four-, or six-cylinder engines. This can cause wear on the engine mounts and stress on the beds, and can throw out the alignment of the engine and shaft. A good part of the sea trial has to do with determining if the alignment is sufficiently smooth. The signs of misalignment include shaft wobble at the stuffing box, excessive noise and vibration, and failure to reach rated r.p.m.

A sea trial will also give the surveyor a chance to see how much water enters the hull via the stuffing box. I am always amazed by how many boats have a serious amount of water entering the bilge from this source. This causes the automatic pumps to work overtime and will run down the battery of a sailboat to

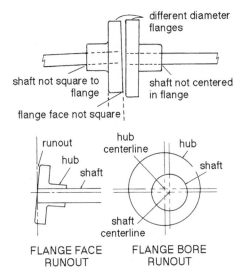

different diameter flanges

shaft not square to flange

shaft not centered in flange

flange face not square

runout

hub centerline

hub

hub

shaft

hub

shaft

shaft

shaft centerline

FLANGE FACE RUNOUT

FLANGE BORE RUNOUT

Cutaway view of the shaft coupling, showing possible causes of misalignment and resulting excessive vibration. The surveyor will recommend that the coupling be opened when excessive vibration is noted at a sea trial. (Courtesy Caterpillar Tractor Co.)

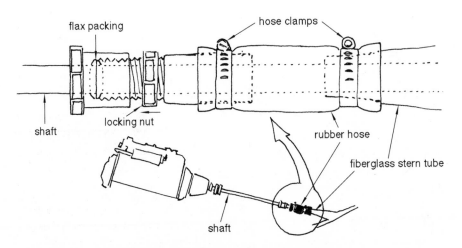

flax packing

hose clamps

shaft

locking nut

shaft

rubber hose

fiberglass stern tube

Stuffing-box assembly. If the stuffing box is dripping, can it be tightened? Check the hose clamps, and inspect the fiberglass stern tube for cracks.

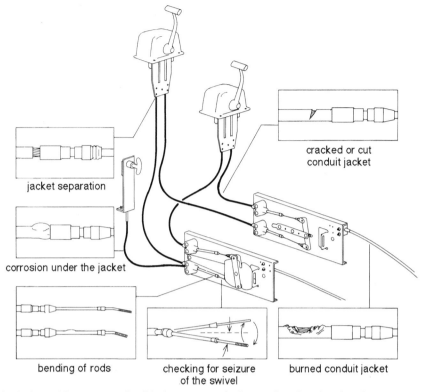

jacket separation

cracked or cut
conduit jacket

corrosion under the jacket

bending of rods

checking for seizure
of the swivel

burned conduit jacket

Single-lever Morse control cable for a transmission or throttle, showing the most common reasons for cable stiffness or failure. Bent rods, jacket separation, and swivel seizure are the most frequent problems. (Courtesy Morse Controls)

the point that the pump cannot cope. (This, by the way, is an argument for not placing a submersible pump at the very bottom of the bilge, where it will be running much of the time.)

During the running period, some surveyors feel the heat exchanger and oil coolers with their hands (in addition to observing the temperature gauge) to determine if they are running too hot. This also is a good time to look for leaks in the cooling system, the fuel delivery system (either

A 12-volt electric fuel pump, common to many diesel engines. These cost about $70, and most diesels will not run without them, especially Universals. It is a good idea to have a spare one aboard!

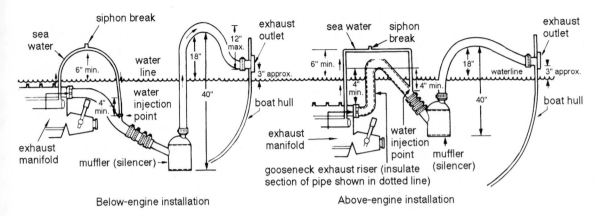

at the lift pump or the secondary pump), oil leaks, exhaust leaks, and leaks in the water injection system for the exhaust.

The surveyor's role stops and the mechanic's begins when engine problems are serious, such as a four-cylinder engine that runs on two or three cylinders, or an engine that cannot reach its rated r.p.m. At this point, the surveyor should advise his client to seek the opinion of a qualified mechanic. Problems identified at survey are almost always accrued to the account of the seller, who either makes a concession in the price of the boat, based on an estimate of repair, or has the problem fixed immediately. After the repair is completed, the surveyor will reinspect the vessel.

Generators

I will confine these remarks to the gasoline and diesel gensets commonly found aboard auxiliary sailing vessels. These are commonly of the 3½ to 20 kw variety, depending on how many accessories the boat has. A generator is a two-piece unit. The first is the engine, and the second is the winding, or generator itself. The surveyor's task is to determine the condition of the engine and to assess whether or not the output is sufficient to carry all the AC loads demanded of it. Modern yachts often are equipped with electric clothes washers and dryers, microwave ovens, reverse-cycle air conditioning and heating systems, televisions, VCR, stereo, large refrigerator/freezer units, and other electric conveniences, plus up to three battery chargers.

Most small craft, including sailing vessels, use 115-volt systems (240 volts in the United Kingdom), with a total capacity of 30 to 50 amps. The generator needs adequate capacity (output), with about 20 percent in reserve, for the total amps that all the boat's AC accessories draw. High-wattage interior lights draw plenty of juice. Three 100-watt light bulbs can draw 30 amps, three air conditioners can easily draw 25 to 30 amps. If you were to use a toaster or hair dryer at the same time as these, you would exceed the capacity of the system and (hopefully) trip the circuit breaker.

Any vessel with a generator needs a voltmeter to measure generator output so that you know what is being provided to the system for distribution to the accessory circuits. An ammeter is also required to monitor the loads, in the aggregate, as you bring them on line. You also should have, in a readily seen position, oil pressure and engine temperature gauges for the generator's engine, preferably with alarm systems for overheating and low oil pressure similar to those on a main engine. A great many small generators are tucked away in a tight corner of the engine room, with the only gauges on the unit itself. The average generator on a sailboat runs about five times more hours than an engine. It is generally a smaller engine and therefore runs at higher r.p.m., so it needs more maintenance than the propulsion engine(s), and certainly more oil and belt changes, pulley replacements, injector servicing, and so on.

The surveyor, with the generator running, inspects the distribution panel, grounds, switches, and breakers, and determines the capacity of the unit (normally from a plate on the generator). After this inspection, all the accessories are brought on line one at a time until the system is carrying as much as it is rated to carry. As the amp draw increases, AC voltage output may drop from 115 VAC to 105 VAC. This is normal, but if it drops much below 100, efficiency will decrease. Most AC units will function to about 90 volts and as high as 125 volts. Any reading lower or higher than this range is cause for concern. Readings of 95 to 100 VAC for an unloaded generator indicate inadequate output. Remember that the unit is in two parts. If the engine is running poorly, it can and will affect the output of the generator. Here again, the surveyor's responsibility is to make a basic performance assessment, report abnormalities during the trials, and to know when to call for an electrician's services.

Pumps and Motors

The average sailboat might have the following pumps: automatic bilge, manual bilge, shower sump, pressure water, saltwater washdown, and holding-tank evacuation or macerator. Larger oceangoing vessels might have, in addition, fuel-transfer pumps and discharges for gray-water and waste holding tanks.

Electric motors include everything from fans to refrigerator compressor motors to blower extractors in the engine room. Motors and pumps are obviously tested where possible, and it is better to test them in a sea trial, because many require seawater to function.

Pumps are rated by gallons per hour (GPH) discharge capacity, and on sailing vessels normally operate on direct current, mostly 12 volt, although 24 volt is not uncommon in a larger auxiliary. There are submersible pumps, such as the bilge pumps made by Rule, and nonsubmersible, such as a PAR diaphragm pump or a centrifugal type such as a Sureflow. Because submersibles operate underwater they have ignition-protected components. Capacities can be as low as 250 GPH in a small unit such as would be suit-

Two types of marine bilge pumps. At left is a submersible Rule pump; at right is a 12-volt nonsubmersible diaphragm pump. While both are dependable, the nonsubmersible types are a bit easier to get at if your boat is large enough to install them above the bilge. Bilge pumps are often installed incorrectly at the factory. You cannot have discharge hoses running directly to ports near the waterline. You must have a loop in the line before it discharges, and the line, if possible, should be angled slightly downward toward the discharge port. You can also vent these loops to guard against siphoning, which is a much more common problem than you might imagine.

able for a shower sump pump, and as high as 5,000 GPH for a lower-bilge installation. Submersible bilge pumps must be installed so that they can be retracted to clean the filter heads, and hoses must be of the noncollapsible type on the intake head, if one is used. Incorrectly installed discharge hoses have caused an alarming number of sinkings in recent years. You cannot run the hose in a straight line to a discharge port, even slightly above the designed waterline, without the distinct possibility of siphoning water back into the boat. I remember a C & C 44 I surveyed that filled up with salt water every time we went sailing, but was entirely dry on the mooring. We could not find any leaks until we noticed that when we were under sail, the stern squatted enough to submerge the discharge port. This immediately started the siphoning action and filled the boat to the floorboards. Moral: The discharge line must have a vented loop, similar to that used in a marine toilet discharge hose, and for the same reason. Further, the location of the discharge port above the designed waterline should include provision for heel angles, motion, and trim of the vessel. No check valves are allowable in a discharge line, because they might jam and prevent discharge of water. The cheap plastic bilge-pump hose commonly used on many production boats is inadequate in my opinion. Good-quality rubber hose is recommended.

Nonsubmersible pumps must be very securely mounted on platforms well away from anticipated high water levels, and they should have ignition-proof wiring. These pumps require a pick-up hose leading into the lower bilge and should always be fitted with a strainer at the head. The PAR pump is useful as a freshwater, saltwater, and bilge pump and can be quickly replaced in a pinch.

Pumps frequently freeze when the boat is laid up in cold climates half the year. Empty them as part of the winterizing by breaking the hose connections, instead of simply running an antifreeze solution into them.

Charging Systems

Most sailing auxiliaries utilize engine-driven alternators to keep the batteries in a good state of charge. When you engage any ship's appliance on the 12-, 24-, or 32-volt system, storage batteries provide the power. The alternator(s) simply keeps the batteries charged. In order for the alternator to charge properly, a rectifier must be placed between the alternator and the battery. The rectifier converts the alternator's AC to the batteries' DC voltage. To test the alternator, attach a multimeter to the storage battery poles while the engine is running (driving the alternator) and note the voltage reading. Standing voltage on a charged battery is about 12.5 to 12.8 volts. With a functional alternator providing a charge, voltage is higher: 13.5 to 14 volts would be about right.

The other component that needs to be in good order is the voltage regulator. Usually, a malfunction here will show up as very high or very low voltage readings. If the voltage begins to spike up or down, the regulator may be at fault. If the voltage stays too high for too long, you will end up cooking your batteries. The electrolyte surrounding the battery plates will literally evaporate. If you notice a rotten-egg odor throughout the boat, this is a good place to start looking for the cause!

Wiring connections at the alternator, the battery selector switch, and the battery pole connections must be clean. The alternator drive belt has to be correctly tensioned—if it's too loose it will slip; if it's too tight, it will cause the alternator pulley bearing to wear out. It should deflect about $\frac{3}{8}$ to $\frac{1}{2}$ inch at its longest span under moderate finger pressure.

All of these simple tests can be done before the boat is launched. Just get a hose to the engine so that you can start up and run for a reasonable time, say 10 minutes. Alternators are pretty dependable, and when they fail it's usually obvious. I recommend rebuilding or exchanging them every five or six years, and it is not a bad idea to make a swap when you buy a used boat so you can have a benchmark. Incidentally, not many boatyards test alternators in the spring commissioning.

Battery Chargers

Battery chargers, or converters, make it possible to recharge storage batteries from shore power or onboard generators. The incoming AC power is stepped down from between 110 and 115 volts (240 volts in the U.K.) to battery voltage (12, 24, or 32 volts), then rectified to direct current using diodes. Most converters presently in service on auxiliary sailboats are regulated to maintain the battery at a constant voltage. When battery voltage falls, the converter increases its output, and vice versa, in the same fashion as an alternator. Most of these units vary in rated output from 20 amps, for one or two batteries, to 60 amps for larger-capacity battery banks (although one would need to know at what voltage the output was rated in order to compare one charger with another). A large yacht with twin engines, generators, etc., might have two or three chargers. The initial output of amps to a discharged battery bank is high, then this level is reduced to a trickle after full charge is attained. Most constant-potential chargers are regulated for 13.8 volts, though any such setting is a compromise. If the setting were higher, the recharge rate would be faster; if it were lower, there would be less risk of overcharging the battery or batteries when the charger is left on for days at a time. (Some chargers maintain a constant current until a threshold battery voltage is reached, then trip to a trickle charge to maintain a lower float voltage—say, 13.2 to 13.6—thus banishing the risk of overcharging, but these converters are much more expensive.) At dockside for a survey, I try to engage the system when I come aboard, then monitor it at midday and again at the end of the day. The reverse method, when the boat has been plugged in with the charger going for two weeks and no significant amps are being generated, is to hydrostatically test the batteries. This confirms that they are at a full level of charge, as indicated by the low rate of charge.

In most small-craft applications, the converter wiring runs from the charger housing along the battery cables and connects to the battery's positive terminal. If these connections get any significant wear at the wire-to-eye fitting, or get very corroded, charging rates will be poor or nonexistent.

Chapter 6

Surveying the Masts and Standing Rigging

In most production fiberglass sailboats, the masts, booms, and spinnaker poles are made from series 6000 extruded aluminum alloys, usually in the 6061 or 6062 designations. Most of these extrusions today are electrochemically treated by anodizing to form a protective coating over the metal and prevent saltwater corrosion and pitting. For the immediate future, aluminum will continue to be the material of choice for masts because of its relatively low cost. Some custom builders are using carbon-fiber masts with good success, as the weight saving aloft improves the stability of a vessel, and I would certainly recommend this for a vessel intended for long-distance sailing if your budget can handle the increased cost.

Masts

If at all possible, masts should be inspected while unstepped. An important stress area at the "partners," the area hidden within the deck collar, cannot be assessed with the column in place, and the "butt" section sitting in the well of the mast-step plate is also difficult to gauge with the mast standing.

What you want to inspect first are the spar sections, or the extruded portions of the mast and boom. These you view for bends, kinks, and cracks. Some masts are sectioned—that is to say they are made in two pieces butt-joined with a sleeve inside, and then mechanically fastened with machine screws or rivets. After noting any problems in this area, move to the masthead plate or crane, which is usually cast aluminum and can be either mechanically fastened or welded. Welding is favored, because aluminum is so sensitive that any type of mechanical fastening (usually stainless steel) is likely to cause some galvanic deterioration in the adjacent aluminum. The masthead plate is also the base for the masthead light and often the VHF antenna bracket and wind-indicator pedestal. All of these are viewed to ensure that they are securely attached and undamaged.

The reason I recommended doing this with the mast unstepped is that the alternative is to do it from a bosun's chair, sometimes 100 feet above decks. This kind of inspection must be done annually in any event; if you must do it from a chair, the absolute minimum nod to safety is to tie a loose line all the way around you and the mast, with a snap shackle that can be opened as you go around the spreaders. This line will jam you against the mast if you fall, and is a lot simpler than rigging an extra halyard. Most experts recommend this safety line *in addition to* two halyards, both of which are made off to the chair bridle with a bowline or screw shackle rather than a snap shackle. Try to enlist two helpers, one for winching and one for tailing the halyard, and do not use a mast winch in the line of fire of any tools you may drop. Instead, run the halyard through a turning block on deck and back to a sheet winch.

Next in line are the masthead sheaves, the rollers on which the halyards turn. These are commonly a very hard plastic, and sometimes aluminum (not a good choice). These sheaves are distorted out of round over time and begin to jam, causing the halyard to slide rather than roll over the surface and eventually to wear out. Make sure the sheaves are undamaged and turning freely. They ride on a stainless steel pin that must be well secured at the ends.

There are commonly two taper welds in the upper 4 to 5 feet of the mast. These allow the mast to be tapered, thus removing some weight aloft. Inspect these for cracks. (A magnifying glass will help on all the close inspections.) While you are at the masthead, note the condition of the forestay and backstay swages and the clevis pins, paying particular care to the swage body. It should be straight on the shank, and no cracks are permissible. The upper swages are not so troublesome as the lowers, as they do not hold water and are less prone to corrosion where the wire enters the swage.

There are one or two spinnaker bails and blocks to be viewed while you are

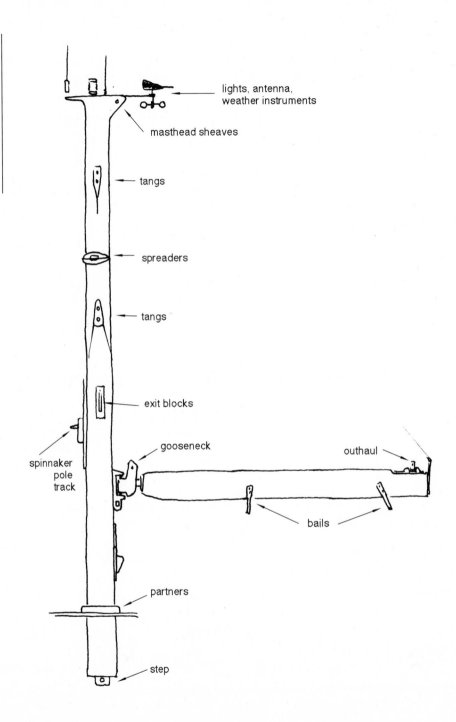

lights, antenna,
weather instruments

masthead sheaves

tangs

spreaders

tangs

exit blocks

gooseneck

outhaul

spinnaker
pole
track

bails

partners

step

Aluminum mast and boom inspection points (dimensions distorted for clarity).

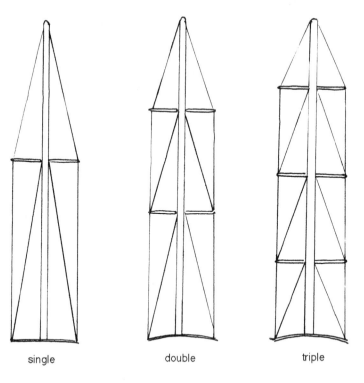

single   double   triple

Single-, double-, and triple-spreader rigs. The latter are used on performance boats, but the idea is the same: the shorter panel sections between spreaders allow the use of a lighter mast, with thinner walls and a smaller diameter. As can be seen, the upper and lower sections of the column are better supported with the double- or triple-spreader rigs. We have, unfortunately, gone a bit too far with this idea at times, with the resulting loss of many rigs that relied too much on the standing rigging and used too light a mast. Though not shown here, spreader tips should be cocked upward to bisect shroud angles.

about it, and if the mast is stepped, have the anchor light engaged to see if it works, and note the condition of the lens cap.

Next in line is the first set of spreaders. As masts have become smaller in diameter and somewhat taller for performance, many cruising boats now have two sets of spreaders. A failure of any spreader to provide lateral support to the mast column puts the section in jeopardy, so the inspection of the spreaders and their mounts is very important. The two critical inspections are at the base, or the part attached to the mast, and the tips, where the wire or rod is attached to prevent the spreader tips from moving up or down. These tips are normally covered by a plastic or rubber boot to pre-

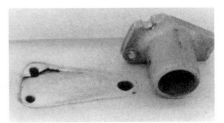

Combination tang and spreader mount of stainless steel, on an aluminum alloy mast. The socket is welded, and the flange is bolted through the mount and tacked with tapping screws. All fittings should be closely inspected for fatigue and weld failure, and the standing rigging swages and pins (also shown here) should be checked.

Broken aluminum alloy spreader socket, which has in turn cracked the alloy mast. (Sally Henderson photo, from Understanding Rigs and Rigging, by Richard Henderson, International Marine, 1990)

vent the ends from chafing the larger genoas during tacks.

There are several methods of attaching spreaders to a mast. One utilizes a fixed bar through the mast section with extensions long enough to fit the hollow spreader over and secure it with a clevis pin. Another is a welded baseplate with integral extension piece. Yet another is a socket, again with a clevis pin to secure the spreader butt. Whichever construction you find, it is much easier to view when disassembled. Where a double-spreader rig is employed, there will be intermediate shrouds, the function of which is to stiffen the upper mast section. These are adjustable with turnbuckles if made of wire, or fixed in length if made of solid rod; but they will always have clevis pins securing the ends, and these and the cotter pins must be in good condition.

Most aluminum masts these days use an internal sail track, but a few still have external tracks. The internal luff channel has to be clear and straight in order not to foul the sail as it is hoisted.

Booms

The boom extrusions or sections are inspected in the same manner as the mast sections, for stress cracks, bends and kinks, corrosion, and condition of fittings. The gooseneck fitting is of particular interest. The plate attached to the mast might be welded, secured with riveting, or fastened with stainless steel machine screws. There will normally be a downhaul adjustment for tensioning the luff, and below the gooseneck there may be a fixed vang, for flattening the mainsail, or a simple manually adjusted preventer. All of these components are inspected for wear or slack and noted by the surveyor. The boom sections have evolved over the years from round to elliptical, and may house lines: the reefing lines, outhaul, and topping lift in a racing boat, somewhat fewer in a cruising boat. A boom is fitted with bails that act as the dead-end for the mainsheet, and as such need to be well secured. One of the annoying problems of modern designs has been the inclination of the designers to move the mainsheet travelers out of the cockpit (for creature comforts), and place them above the companionway sliding hatch. This does not allow for a good sheeting angle, often taking the strain at the midpoint of the boom. Consequently, a number of booms have failed and bent or cracked under extreme loads. This is quite common in J-boats. This type of arrangement is certainly not suitable for extended offshore use.

Hydraulic boom vangs cause some interesting failures, typically at the underside of the boom where the vang plate is welded. The weld may also fail at the connection on the lower end of the mast, but this is not so frequent in my experience.

Standing Rigging

Now we get to the meat of the rigging—the shrouds, headstays, and backstays, with their bearing loads on the chainplates. The common wire of choice is 1 x 19 stainless steel with stainless swages on the end fittings. The upper swages and pins need to be inspected for cracks, tightness of clevis pins, and presence and snugness of cotter pins. Next the stranded wire is inspected for burrs (affectionately known as "meathooks") or unraveling strands. At the deck, the swages are mated to turn-buckles, which are in turn mated to a toggle pinned through a chainplate. All of these connections need to be in good repair to protect the integrity of the rig.

The upper deadends of the shrouds are called tangs; these are stainless flat bars through-bolted to the mast, to which the upper swages are pinned. The current fashion on many racer/cruiser designs is to take the uppers and lowers to a single chainplate rather than run the lowers to separate plates, but this is not a suitable rig for an offshore boat in my opinion simply because it is not as strong as the divided shrouds. Stay and shroud chainplate stresses were discussed in Chapter 2.

The three particular problem areas to look for in rod rigging are a straight crack in the rod itself, a failure in the cold heads that connect the rod to the turnbuckles, and a crack in the angled sections that pass over the spreader tips. Rod as a general rule

A shroud tang improperly aligned. When the shroud is under tension, the force is transferred to the corner of the pin, rather than the entire pin. The wire will also apply stress to the swage fitting as it pulls unfairly. (from Understanding Rigs and Rigging, *by Richard Henderson, International Marine, 1990)*

has surveyed well for me, and it does stay tuned better than wire. Discontinuous rod shrouds, which are not bent over the spreader tips but rather are comprised of sections mated at the spreaders, wear longer and better.

Reefing/Furling Systems and Hydraulics

Certainly one of the more difficult areas of a survey for me is evaluating the wire inside a *luff foil,* which is the aluminum extrusion that fits around a stay in a roller reefing system. You just cannot see the condition of the wire, except perhaps at the swages. In a typical roller reefing headsail system, the foil is fitted in linked sections over the headstay; a swivel is fitted at the head of the

The Harken headsail furling device. Inspection of these units includes the drum furler (bottom), the toggle and clevis pin at the tack, and the two upper swivels, which have ball bearings. Some systems substitute Teflon bushings for bearings, and these do wear out, causing slack, which in turn can cause the swivels to bind. The last area of inspection is the extruded aluminum luff foil, which covers the headstay. The foil has two, three, or four interlocking sections, depending on the length of the stay. These can break, twist, or elongate, and the sail tracks in the foils need to be straight and clear.

sail, and a furling drum at the tack. On the upper part of the rig there are three important connecting fittings to be viewed: the stay swage and pin at the masthead, the halyard shackle at the top of the swivel, and the shackle holding the head of the sail to the bottom of the swivel. The three important lower end fittings are the tack shackle, the swage to the top of the drum furler, and of course the hardware connecting the drum to the stemhead.

Hydraulic backstays are common today. This is unfortunate, as I think the benefits derived from better sailing performance are outweighed by the stress they cause on hulls and rigs. Manual adjustment is a bit slower but accomplishes the same thing (headstay sag reduction) more safely.

A hydraulic system includes a ram, a hose, and a fluid reservoir. Pressure fittings are needed on the hose, obviously, and the surveyor should inspect these for leaks. There is a pressure bleed to reduce tension, and this too has to be in working order. Most units have a pressure gauge; engaging the system to 500 pounds per square inch and watching the gauge hold the pressure will give you a good idea how the system is working. The level of the fluid in the reservoir should also be checked. Leaks are easily spotted from fluid traces. The carrying hoses, much like seacock hoses, develop brittleness and cracks when they need replacing.

A Navtec hydraulic backstay cylinder, integral with the backstay. The handle supplies the force to move the ram. A reservoir (not shown) supplies the hydraulic fluid. A pressure gauge notes the desired level. All connections have to be inspected, all pressure lines inspected for leaks, and the pressure and relief functions tested.

One of the reasons I don't like hydraulics, aside from the stress imparted to hull and rig, is what happens when pressure is released and not enough pressure is maintained on the backstay. As the unsupported mast whips forward and aft, the mast section at the deck level (the partners) is alternately in tension or compression, and it can and will crack if this slack is not corrected. These systems can be fitted with a check in the line that prevents tension from being entirely relieved, and I recommend this safeguard.

Hydraulic vangs, as I mentioned, put tremendous stress on welds and the boom sections and are better left to racing boats, where the risk of this sort of damage is deemed acceptable.

Running Rigging

Running rigging includes halyards, running backstays, spinnaker sheets and guys, sheets for sail control, downhauls, outhauls, reefing gear, topping lift, mechanical vangs, and any other piece of rigging that moves. Most of it is braided polyester (Dacron in the U.S., Terylene in the U.K.) except perhaps in very small daysailers, which might use some three-strand laid polyester. It wears out more from chafe than age, and certain items go faster than others.

Internal halyards chafe on sheaves at the masthead and on through-bolts inside the mast and at exit blocks. Sheets chafe on genoa-track cars, blocks, and from constant winching action, among other things, but being larger in diameter than most other running rigging, they can last a good long time. Braided Dacron will last almost indefinitely if it is not cut through. In order to get a proper view of running rigging, you need to run it out where you can see it full length. Other considerations are the condition of the splices to all shackle fittings and the fittings themselves. The spinnaker-pole track, car, and bail are also part of this inspection, along with the pole end fitting and snap releases.

Chapter 7

The Role of the Surveyor

Of all the surveyor's responsibilities, his best is acting as a prospective buyer's advocate in the negotiations leading to the purchase of a yacht. In this role, the surveyor inspects and comments on all facets of the vessel under consideration. These include the suitability of the boat for the intended use of the buyer, the resin system used, quality control of the construction, and detailed inspections of the hull, deck, rig, and machinery. After inspection, he gives his opinion of the boat's market value.

A purchase-and-sale agreement should always include the provision for a marine survey, giving the prospective buyer the option to reject a boat and get a refund of his moneys, or renegotiate the purchase price, if serious flaws are found. If you require a loan to make the purchase, be sure to make the agreement contingent on securing suitable financing, and establish a mutually agreed date by which the survey will be completed and financing obtained. Generally fourteen business days is adequate.

The array of forces in the buyer/seller exchange typically breaks down like this: Buyer and surveyor on one side, broker and seller on the other. Each party is motivated differently. The buyer wants to get the best boat he can for his money; the seller wants as near his asking price as he can get; and the broker wants to make a fair commission on the sale. The broker has a difficult time, because he starts out representing the seller (listing the seller's boat), then he locates a buyer and has to negotiate a price that's acceptable to both. After the survey, he may have to renegotiate the price to reflect what the surveyor has found to be a *priority repair.* At this point, the fur usually flies; deals are made or lost. The key question is, "What constitutes a priority repair?"

The answer is any listed piece of equipment that does not function in the manner for which it was designed; any system necessary to the everyday operation of a vessel; any section of a hull, deck, rudder, or rigging damaged or deemed unsuitable for the intended use of a vessel (as understood by the surveyor in his presurvey discussion with the buyer); National Fire Protection Association (NFPA) or Coast Guard recreational boat code violations; and any major engine flaws. The key phrase here is "intended use." A certain amount of stress-induced hull and deck damage is tolerable if the surveyor knows that the boat will be used as a weekend cruiser in coastal waters. The same boat, if used offshore, might not be suitable.

It is over the intended-use question that many surveyors and brokers part company. I know of many brokers who feel it is none of the surveyor's business what the buyer wants to do with a boat, and they would appreciate it if the surveyor kept quiet and simply listed the malfunctioning systems and structurally important items. Another sore point is a surveyor's commenting on the placement of systems in a vessel, including components that may have been put where they are by the factory (as if that made everything all right!). I remember surveying a Bristol 35.5 in Marblehead a few years ago. It was a very nice boat, cosmetically excellent, with good workmanship in the laminates, and its engine and rig in good shape, but the builders had placed the domestic water heater in the sail locker in a way that totally impeded access to the stuffing box. I recommended on the survey that the heater be moved to another location, and the buyer asked for a reduction in price that reflected this cost. I have not had a survey from that broker since! I try to remind myself, constantly, that if a stuffing box lets go, and for some reason the boat founders, it is not the broker's name the underwriters see on the survey report. It's mine.

Is there collusion between some brokers and some surveyors? You bet there is. I know of a brokerage that uses one surveyor who does not have any certifications whatsoever and has been in the business five or six years. The reason the brokerage uses him is that he soft-peddles serious problems to the buyers and does not get into design problems or intended-use interpretations. He makes $20,000 a year from one firm. The problem with his approach is that it doesn't do much on behalf of the buyer, who, if he ever buys another boat, won't use this surveyor a second time.

So how do you, the owner/buyer, find a surveyor on your own? The best way is to get in touch with one of the professional surveying associations. There are two U.S. surveying associations: the National Association of Marine Surveyors (NAMS), P.O. Box 9306, Chesapeake, VA 23321-9306, 1-800-822-NAMS; and the Society of Accredited Marine Surveyors, 1-800-SAMS. The membership of these associations totals some 1,600. The estimated number of part-time/noncertified surveyors is about 7,000. Marine surveying is a totally unregulated profession, unfettered by state or federal supervision. This means that anyone can hang out a shingle tomorrow and get right into it! The only regulation offered is through these professional associations, which can censure and expel members, but they cannot prevent them from continuing to survey. They hold regional seminars, which are designed to keep members current on Coast Guard regulations, fire-protection compliance regulations, new building techniques, repairs, osmosis treatments, and a host of other topics ranging from stability tests to maritime law. They give their members a uniform method of survey practices and approaches that will provide a prospective buyer with a thorough survey. This is better for a buyer than just picking anyone out of the Yellow Pages. In addition, these organizations have criteria for membership, generally including documented proof of time in the profession, and may require written testing before full certification is granted. There are grades of membership—apprentice, associate, and full membership—of which you should take note before you select a surveyor. Banks and insurance companies generally also keep lists of surveyors they recommend, as will yacht brokers.

NAMS was formed in New York in 1962. I am a full member and certified by them to practice. This designation is CMS (certified marine surveyor), which apprentices and associates are not permitted to use. SAMS was formed in the late 1980s. To my knowledge, this association uses roughly the same guidelines as NAMS.

Some surveyors are designated to perform work for the classification societies, such as Bureau Veritas and Lloyds, and a qualification in this respect is a good indication of a well-rounded surveyor. If you need a survey of a boat located in Europe or England, you may want to select a surveyor who belongs to a surveying association in that part of the world, because his reports would be readily accepted by underwriters there.

How much experience should a surveyor have? After some thought about this, I think that 10 years or more is desirable. This amount of time should indicate that the person has surveyed all forms of hull construction—fiberglass, steel, aluminum, and wood—and is competent to survey each type. Most surveyors with less than 10 years' experience are limited to fiberglass.

I have found that it is sometimes difficult to ascertain what real experience is. One surveyor advertises he has 30 years of marine experience, which in translation means he has been surveying for three years, but worked in a boatyard for the other 27. So the key here is *surveying experience*, not just general experience. I divide surveyors into four grades: incompetent, semicompetent, competent, and very, very good. The first two categories are generally associates or apprentices; the latter two are generally members of at least one recognized surveying body.

Assuming you find several candidates with some or all of the qualifications, take the time to talk with the ones on your short list, and find the one who you feel most understands your intended use of a boat and the systems you require.

Types of Surveys

Many specialty areas of surveying have nothing to do with representing buyers. These include surveys of cargo, marina facilities, drydocks, and damage, to mention several. Most surveyors specialize to some degree. Many, like myself, are hull and machinery types, generally any tonnage in commercial or pleasure craft. Ships are done by classification surveyors. Barges, however, are often done by small-craft surveyors, and some surveyors work more in commercial vessels than others. The specialty chosen by the surveyor is usually dictated by what type of work is available in a given area. Here are the principal types of surveys and brief descriptions of their purposes.

Prepurchase

This type of survey is done on behalf of a prospective buyer, and includes inspection of the entire vessel—machinery, systems, safety gear, inventory. It also includes a haulout inspection, and, if possible, a sea trial. Reports run 12 to 20 pages, depending on the size of the vessel, and state the market and replacement values for the insurance companies and lenders.

Condition and Value

This is a much misunderstood term these days. Insurance companies used to ask for this type of survey on policy renewals. The surveyor's task was to visit the boat and determine if the owners were properly looking after it, and whether it was still, in the surveyor's opinion, worth what it was being covered for in the policy. It was, in other words, the equivalent of a quick once-over. But the condition and value survey now more closely approaches the prepurchase survey in scope and detail, but without the sea trials. It may sometimes be done in the water, however.

Damage Surveys

Here the surveyor, as in the C & V survey, works at the behest of the insurance carrier, who has engaged him to assess the extent and cause of damage to a vessel. Determinations include the time, date, and circumstances of the "adventure," as they like to call it, the cause if it can be ascertained, and a detailed estimate of the

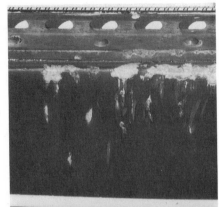

What neglect can do. This boat was left tied to a barge during a Boston Harbor gale, and it took a pounding.

repairs. The report, with photos, is forwarded to the underwriters, who determine whether the casualty, based on the surveyor's report, is repairable or a total loss.

Voyage Surveys

There are not too many of these being done anymore, but an underwriter for whom a surveyor has performed a prepurchase survey on a particular vessel may ask him to examine the credentials of the captain, engineer, and crew before the vessel makes a transatlantic voyage. Included in this would be an inspection of the detailed route, approved by the underwriters; the fuel capacity and other oceangoing provisions; ship's documents; and safety gear.

On-Off Hire Inspections

These generally are done when a commercial vessel has been leased for a particular period of time. The surveyor makes an inspection before the hire commences and again after the completion of the lease to note any damages to the vessel, which are then negotiated between the two parties.

Following are examples first of a prepurchase survey and second, a condition and value survey. Note the differences in content and scope.

Prepurchase Survey

Date of survey: 12/08/92

Personal & Confidential
For: Mr. Tom Rankin
105 Hemlock Drive
E. Greenwich, R.I.

Report of Survey 41' auxiliary ketch *Wandering Star*
Type: Island Trader 41'

H.I.N. ETY 410141177
Document No. N/A
Engine: Westerbeke Diesel
Type of survey: Prepurchase, hauled

Scope of Survey

Moisture and percussion tests of hull and deck laminates, osmosis inspection, visuals of keel, ballast and rudder, shafting and propeller, cathodic protection. Visuals of teak decking, ports, hatches, rails, mast collars as visible, interior structural bulkheads and stiffeners, steering gear. Twelve-volt navigational systems engaged insofar as possible, ship's pumps and systems engaged insofar as possible. Mast and rigging viewed from aloft, sails viewed in bags. The engine and machinery were serviced and started by Brewers Yacht Yard, Wickford, and winterized after running for 20 minutes, no loads. No oil samples were requested or drawn.

At the request of Mr. Rankin, the above-named surveyor did attend the vessel *Wandering Star* as she lay hauled out at Wickford Cove Marina, on December 8, 1992. The purpose of this survey was to ascertain the condition of the hull and deck laminates, spars, rigging, machinery, and electrical systems, and to prepare an estimate for repairs necessary to the principal systems of the vessel. The prospective buyer attended the survey.

Principal Specifications
Builder: Marine Trading International, Taiwan
Year built: 1977
Model: Island Trader 41' ketch
LOA: 41'3"
Beam: 12'6"
Draft: 6'
Displacement: approx. 28,000 lbs.
Ballast: Internal cast or other.
Hull color: White, teak overlay decks.
Engine: approx. 50-h.p. Westerbeke diesel,
Hurth reduction.

Construction
   Solid laminate GRP hull, using polyester
resins. Decks are balsa-cored GRP, with teak
overlay. Deckhouse trim is teak, rails are
teak. Masts are Sitka spruce, rigging is
stainless wire.

Hull and Deck Inspection
   Found this vessel in poor cosmetic condition,
mainly from neglect. She is stored outside and
uncovered, and has been laid up for some 12 to
18 months I understand.
   Inspection of the exterior hull shows minor
gelcoat damage, chips, and abrasions on the
stem, the midpoint of the keel, and under the
port bow where an old gelcoat repair was poorly
finished. There is some caprail damage on the
starboard side, about 12 feet abaft the bow,
where a scarf repair will be necessary to the
teak rail. Farther aft, also to starboard, is a
cracked section of teak that should be upgraded.
The condition of the bottom paint is poor,
mostly flaked off at this point, and this will
require sanding and preparation before new
antifouling is applied. There is some fastening
bleeding from the chainplate attachments on the
topsides that can be cleaned off.
   On deck, all brightwork surfaces are in poor
condition. This includes rails, hatches, trim
pieces, pinrails, and the cosmetic condition of
the teak decks. Everything needs to be

upgraded. A grabrail on the port side of the raised section of the trunk cabin is adrift and broken. Adjacent to this rail is a small area of stress crazing on the nonskid blue deck.

Inspection of the deck hatches and portlights shows them to be in generally good repair. Some gasket renewal will help any minor leaks. The opening and fixed ports looked to be strong and in good repair. Inspection of the bow rail, lifelines, and stanchions shows them in good condition, well secured and without stress. The lifelines are showing some wear under the holes and should be wrapped. The bow platform and sprit were noted to be in good repair.

The deck and cockpit are teak overlaid; the strips are about 5/16 to 3/8 inch and are adequately caulked. There is no lifting at this time, and they appear well secured. I recommend renewing the caulking seal around the cabin and cockpit, under the trim piece, which is loose in spots and leaks into the quarter berth from the starboard cockpit and sidedeck areas. The lazarette and cockpit lockers and seats appear in adequate condition.

Hull and deck surfaces were percussion tested for delaminations or voids and no unusual areas were noted. Hull and deck appear to be well laid up.

Moisture tests, using the Protimeter Aquant instrument, do not show unusually high concentration of moisture in the hull or deck laminates. Hull averages 105 to 106, topsides 103 to 104, decks 102. All of these are within the acceptable range. The bottom and sidewall fiberglass of the ballast cavity were closely inspected and do not show any swelling or serious grounding damage that would indicate any water in the cavity.

The rudder is an attached type with straps and a heel casting, all of which are in good repair at this time. There is some minor pitting corrosion at the heel, which is protected by a zinc anode and copper strapping. The strap has deteriorated and should be renewed. The bar zinc and the shaft zinc are to be renewed as well.

Percussion of the rudder indicates it is a solid laminate and is in good condition at this time. A small split at the inner edge near the bottom of the join line should be sealed.

The rudder radius is normal, turns easily, and the stainless post appears in good condition. Heel casting and pin are secure. The stainless shafting was noted to be in good condition; the water-lubricated Cutless bearing is showing some wear and should be replaced this year or next. The propeller is a three-bladed fixed type, blades and hub in good condition. No scale or damage noted. Size not noted.

Inspection of the exterior portions of the seacocks shows some greenish tinge that may indicate electrochemical reaction on the starboard aft discharges below the waterline. I would check the bonding system carefully. The main grounding system for the engine was not in good repair, which may account for this. The remaining units were well bedded and without corrosion. Strainers were well secured.

Interior Inspection

The interior inspection was made to encompass the following areas: hull-to-deck joint, structural and secondary bulkheads, hull stringers, ballast covering, and tankage.

Where visible, the hull-to-deck joint appears secure and for the most part dry. The bulkheads are marine plywood and were inspected for the condition of the tabs holding them to the hull shell, and the condition of the wood itself. The chainlocker, main, secondary, and aft bulkheads were found in good repair and holding adequately. There is some weakening in the shower stall forward bulkhead that requires attention. This is an area of 1 x 1 foot.

The hull stiffeners, where visible, appear to be in good condition—I saw no signs of stress. The ballast covering is heavy rovings of cloth, well sloped aft toward the main bilge, and appears dry and in good condition. There are two steel fuel tanks located in the bilge, and both have been doused in salt water. Both tanks will have to be thoroughly cleaned, filters dumped, exterior surfaces repainted because rust has begun. They appear structurally sound at this time and are well secured. The fill hoses are showing some wear and should be renewed fairly soon. Vents are adequate, and all fuel manifold valves are working.

The aft bulkhead, which encompasses a quarter berth and the storage area for the LPG tanks, hot-water systems, and refrigeration compressor motor, is unfinished and stripped. Here there is some water damage around an opening port that needs to be upgraded, and the finished covering boards need to be framed in.

The main cabin sole was also covered with salt water and will require cleaning, prepping, and revarnishing. The vertical surfaces are in fairly good condition.

Inspection of the mast-step area for the main indicates this is in good repair as far as can be viewed with the spar in place. The collar section does not show any stress. The mizzen step, however, is deflecting downward 2 to 3 inches, and when the masts are removed for revarnishing, the step area will need to be evaluated and reinforced.

There is some water trace around the forward cabin hatch, which should be properly sealed and gasketed.

Two stainless steel water tanks were noted placed under the settee berths, port and starboard. Both are well secured and chocked. The delivery lines and vents are original and appear secure.

Inspection of the sea valves below the water-line showed a number of rusted hose clamps, or single clamps, which should be replaced and doubled. I am told that these valves were pulled apart and greased, but several were difficult to operate, including two in the WC (head) under the sink. Review all valves.

There is a fair amount of scum and mildew in various lockers and bilge areas to be cleaned and painted.

Ship's 12-Volt Systems, Pumps, and Motors

The saltwater dousing seems to have disabled most of these systems. The electric bilge pump, the freshwater pump, and the shower sump pumps are inoperative and appear frozen. I recommend these be replaced with new equipment. The 12-volt wiring runs in the bilge are to be replaced; the 110-volt outlet runs should be tested and any connections renewed as necessary.

The main electrical panel is a breaker type. At least four switches are inoperative, and I would like to see all of these replaced, because the panel is 15 years old. Much of the 12-volt wiring in the bilge is unmarked and should be identified as to function. All old wiring should be removed.

On the 110-volt side, the converter unit is inoperative at survey. The inlet plug is also burned, and I would inspect the plug inlet wiring to ABYC standards.

Many of the systems that were not working may be wiring-related rather than equipment failures, but this will have to be ascertained by the electrician as he goes through the system. The main cabin interior lights, the Signet navigational systems, the Loran, the stereo, the radar, the refrigeration compressor, and the ship's running lights are inoperative. The stern light fitting has been removed and will need to be replaced.

The following 12-volt ship's systems were operational but will need wiring maintenance as well: autopilot, VHF radio, aft cabin lights, forward cabin lights.

As mentioned, all the ship's pumps were inoperative.

Machinery Inspection

A four-cylinder Westerbeke diesel of approximately 50 h.p. with a Hurth reduction gearing is freshwater cooled and installed under the galley structure. Access to packing glands and for overall maintenance is very good. Oil sump and gear fluids were topped off and clean. This engine was immersed in salt water, and was pickled by Wickford Cove Marina. I understand that it has been flushed and fluids changed as necessary. For survey, the fuel system was bypassed to avoid contaminated diesel. The engine started easily and appears to run smoothly, considering it had not been run for some time. The idle is good, run-up is good. No leaks were noted in the cooling system or the fuel-delivery system. The starter and alternator are newly installed, no hours. The raw-water cooling pump is also new. The exhaust system is a water-injected type, piping in good repair. Muffler is a fiberglass Aqualift in good repair, and the reinforced hoses are in adequate condition. The looped portion of the riser is threaded pipe, and this should be heat-wrapped. The exterior painted surfaces of the engine are poor and need to be detailed. Inspection of the engine beds and mounts shows them in serviceable condition. The shaft coupling was viewed and found in good repair, wired closed. The stuffing-box clamps should be renewed. Alignment should be checked after launch, and all packing glands adjusted for flow then. There are adequate filters and water separators in the system. The main-engine control cables are not attached at the helm end. I was told that these are not good, but cannot comment on them myself. They may be stiff on the engine side and unusable. The control is a single-lever Morse type, which is in working condition. The cable bracket is rusty.

Mast and Rigging Inspection

This is a ketch rig, with spruce or similar mainmast and mizzenmast, and both booms are wood. Both masts are keel stepped. The masts, booms, and spreaders need to be stripped and revarnished immediately. Both booms have had repairs at the gooseneck sections, which were done with fiberglass wraps where splitting occurred. These may require additional reinforcement, because there is some rot present in the main boom at this area. The end pieces of both booms also show some splitting and rot.

I inspected the mainmast from aloft and found the main section in good condition. Some minor wooding here and there will help. The port spreader had rot at the base connection, and both spreaders had lost all UV protection. Noted the halyards operate very stiffly, and I suspect the sheaves are binding. This should be attended to while they are out for varnishing. The condition of the standing rigging is pretty good. This is heavy gauge 1 x 19 wire with swaged ends. The swages were free of cracks and generally straight. There are three sets of shrouds, with no major kinks or unravelings of wire. The rigging pins should be upgraded all around. Tangs and through-bolts appear in good condition. A main-halyard reel winch is in working order. The other deck winches are stiff and require service. The mizzenmast was inspected from the deck only. It requires wooding at the lower section where some cracks are opening up.

Turnbuckles are in good repair, the flat bar chainplate extrusions on deck appear in good repair, and are well secured inside the vessel. There are several bleeding spots on the forward chainplates to be cleaned up (on the hull surface). There is an archaic furling system of the Schaefer loose-luff type that will not be a very efficient one for this boat. I recommend you convert this to a Harken or similar good-quality system.

Navigational Systems Viewed
Compass 6" pedestal type
King 8001 Loran-C receiver
Raytheon radar
Signet wind direction and speed
Data Marine depth (new, not installed)
VHF radio

Safety Gear
3 type BC 5-lb. dry chemical extinguishers,
    discharged
6 Type II PFDs
Horn

Horseshoe ring
Flares
1 inflatable dinghy (not inflated)
1 canister raft (needs to be inspected and
    recertified)
Man-overboard (MOB) pole

Steering Gear

Edson bronze gear, wire-to-quadrant pedestal type, with packing gland on shaft. A Cetec Benmar autopilot is chain driven to an additional bronze quadrant. This unit is working.

The steering cable is small in my opinion and is too short; a loop splice has been made at the adjusting eyes. I would replace this system with larger wire. System also needs grease. Sheaves are well secured, pedestal-base idler plate appears in good repair, system operates smoothly. Tension is adequate.

Stove and LPG Tanks

The LPG (liquid pressurized gas) system appears to fuel both the stove and a demand water heater. The heater was not engaged, because the pressure water pump is down, and the system has been winterized. I expect it works well enough and appears in good condition.

The LPG tanks are contained in a stainless locker under the cockpit, and properly vented overboard. There is a regulator but no gauge or solenoid switch, which should be added to the system. The piping and hosing appeared in good condition. The stove and oven were lit and working. Test the gas heater system when commissioned.

The diesel-fired cabin heater in the main cabin appears well installed and heat-protected, and the fuel lines were in good repair. Because this was connected to the main fuel system, it will not be tested until clean fuel is available.

Valuations

Cost New 1977: $65,000
Market Value: $37,500 as is.
Replacement Cost: $120,000

Items Noted for Repair & Compliance

Compliance:

Attend all firefighting equipment, and recertify the canister raft, test the inflatable raft.

Update flares

Install pressure gauge and solenoid for LPG stove.

Priority Items

1. Repair broken sections of starboard caprail.
2. Refurbish quarter berth and aft bulkhead and overhead liner in the cabin.
3. Make necessary repairs to the weak sections of both booms, and grave (replace) or reinforce sections of rot as noted, also on port spreader.
4. Varnish both masts and booms.
5. Clean and repaint both fuel tanks, upgrade fills and vents.
6. Repair the deflected mizzenmast step plate.
7. Remove and replace all 12-volt wiring in bilge. Test all 110-volt wiring in bilge and upgrade as necessary.
8. Replace all circuit switches in main 12-volt panel. Check the 110 VAC inlet plug and wiring to panel for breaker compliance.
9. Rebuild battery-box platform, provision for 4 storage batteries.
10. Replace the shift and throttle cables.
11. Replace the broken port grabrail on raised section of the house.
12. Replace all ship's pumps—water damaged: freshwater, shower sump, bilge.
13. Test radar, Loran, and refrigeration units when wiring completed on 12-volt side. Test Signet systems. Test all interior and running lights after wiring completed. Install sternlight on bracket.
14. Test constavolt (converter) system and outlets on 110 VAC when wiring completed.
15. Detail engine paint and tune engine as recommended by yard.
16. Steering cables to be replaced.
17. Remove and rebed the margin piece of trim

for the teak decks; leaking at the cockpit corner, starboard side. Do all.
18. Reattach all bonding straps. Renew engine ground cable, all battery cables.

Other Items
1. All deck varnish to be upgraded.
2. Teak deck to be cleaned and oiled.
3. Window and hatch seals to be upgraded.
4. Lifelines worn under stanchions.
5. Cabin sole to be revarnished.
6. Bonding strap on bar zinc to be replaced.
7. Shaft zinc to be replaced.
8. Moderate wear on Cutless bearing, renew.
9. Provision for holding tank?
10. Fill gelcoat chips on stem, keel, and under port bow.
11. Seal stress cracks on top of house by traveler.
12. Install Data Marine depth unit.
13. Transducer block loose on hull (old system).
14. Knotmeter paddle is stiff.
15. Prepare and repaint bottom.

With the above items repaired or complied with, the surveyor recommends this vessel as a good marine and fire risk at the values stated above. I recommend a reinspection after work is completed for a change in market value.

Condition and Value Survey

Date of survey: 6/11/90

Personal & Confidential
For: Mr. and Mrs. John Eskesen
45 Beach Bluff Road
Swampscott, MA

Report of Survey
Inknowvation

Type: Tartan 27 Auxiliary Sloop
Year: 1978
H.I.N. TAR 27673M78H
Engine Serial# 31A300964 Diesel 12 h.p.
Document No. N/A
Where surveyed: Hauled at residence
Type of inspection: Condition and Value

At your request, this firm did attend the vessel *Inknowvation* as she lay hauled out at
Swampscott, Massachusetts, for the purpose of
ascertaining the condition and value of the
hull, electronics, and safety equipment. The
machinery was not run. The mast and boom were
viewed unstepped. The electrical system was
tested.

Principal Specifications
Builder: Tartan Marine, Ohio
Year: 1978
Model: T-27
LOA: 27'
Beam: 8'8"
Draft: CB 3'2" up
Displacement: 7,400 lbs.
Hull color: dark blue, white deck

Construction
Solid laminate fiberglass hull, polyester
resins, balsa-cored deck. Full keel and
attached rudder. Aluminized mast and boom sections.

Hull and Deck Inspection

Found the hull and deck in good overall condition, above average for the age of the vessel, and showing good maintenance.

Inspected the seacocks and found all to be the ball-valve type, working freely and well bedded. Hoses and clamps in good repair.

Found no exterior damage, above or below the waterline, and the antifouling paint in good condition. Noted there is no cathodic protection affixed to the propeller shaft. This is to be done before launching to protect against galvanic action or electrolysis.

Found the deck laminates strong and free of stress indications, the portlights and hatches in good repair, and secure. Found the deck hardware, rails, and stanchions and lifelines in good repair.

Inspected the mast step and found it well supported with the collar in good condition.

The interior structural and secondary bulkheads were inspected and found securely tabbed, and the partial hull liner or pan in good condition. The chainplates are secured to internal knees that are through-bolted and without stress indications. The rudder was in good repair, well secured at heel and with the upper bushing tight. Steering is by tiller. The ruddertube was free of stress damage.

Tankage Viewed

One plastic water tank with adequate fills and vents, well chocked and strapped.

Fuel tank is aluminum alloy, welds and hoses in good repair, ventilation good. Well chocked and strapped in the outboard locker.

Rigging Inspection

Found the mast and boom in good condition. No stress or cracking in the main sections, all welds holding. The single set of spreaders was in good repair. The standing rigging is 1 x 19 wire with swaged end fittings, all in good repair. No corrosion present at the mast butt plate. Interior wiring appears in good order. Gooseneck fitting and reefing gear in good repair. The running rigging is Dacron braid. The splices are holding, and the braid is in good overall condition.

Sail Inventory—Not Viewed

Machinery Spaces

A 12-h.p. diesel was installed, with the mounts and beds in good condition. The exhaust is seawater cooled and appears in good repair, including the muffler and hoses. A saltwater strainer is affixed in-line, and adequate fuel filters are in-line. A manual shutoff is at the tank end. The fuel lines are copper pipe and flex hose.

There is adequate ventilation of the machinery spaces, but I didn't see a blower.

Electrical Systems

Twelve-volt ship's service, 110 VAC shore power. The 12-volt system consists of two 12-volt storage batteries, boxed and secured in the starboard sail locker. There is a single battery-selector switch in good repair. The interior and running lights were tested and in good condition. The wiring is color-coded and done to acceptable ABYC codes. The 110 VAC was not tested.

The main distribution panel is a fused type, in good condition. A fused electric bilge pump is fitted and working.

Safety Equipment Viewed
Flares
1 Horseshoe ring
6 Type II PFDs
Bell & horn
First-aid kit
2 Dry chemical fire extinguishers, new

Nav Equipment
Horizon VHF radio
Compass

Data Marine depthsounder
Signet speed & log

Miscellaneous Systems Tested
Manual water pump—OK
Electric bilge—OK
Toilet—OK
Alcohol stove—OK
Centerboard—Could not test on cradle

Valuations
Cost new $30,000
Market value $20,000
Replacement cost Not mfg.

Items Noted for Repair
Compliance—None
Priority Repairs—None

Other Repairs and Recommendations
1. Replace the centerboard wire cable next season. Inspect the pendant when launched this
   season.
2. Remove the centerboard pin caps and inspect
   the steel pin next season before launch.
   Replace if scored.
3. Replace one interior light bulb main cabin.
4. Test mast lights.
5. Install a zinc anode on the end of the propeller shaft before launch this season.
6. Double-clamp all hoses to sea valves below
   waterline.

   With the items above repaired or complied
with, the surveyor recommends this vessel as a
good marine risk at the stated values herein.
Normal navigational limits apply: Eastport,
Maine, to Block Island, Rhode Island.
   The surveyor warrants that this report is a
true and unbiased opinion of the vessel
Inknowvation at the time it was inspected. No
warranties are expressed or implied with the
report, and acceptance of it recognizes this
agreement between all parties concerned.

Survey Fees and Other Costs

U.S. surveyors tend to charge by the running foot, while English surveyors charge on a square-footage basis, length x width.

Although the basic charges are generally very similar among surveyors—let us say between $12.50 and $15 per foot on vessels over 40 feet, and perhaps $10 to $12.50 under 40 feet—the fine print determines how much you will spend. Some Florida surveyors charge time and mileage to and from a job, generally $.30 a mile plus $25 per hour, and others may surcharge the sea trial at a flat rate of, say, $65, in addition to the quoted footage figure. Then there is the matter of the engine survey. As I mentioned, the surveyor may or may not elect or be qualified to do the engine survey. I favor a flat rate that includes travel, sea trial, and the machinery part of the survey. It makes for a fairly high footage rate, but there are no other expenses, and the client knows exactly what the cost is up front.

Let's use as an example a 40-foot C & C undergoing survey 100 miles from the surveyor's base. He quotes $12.50 per foot for the job. This is $500 for the boat. He then adds $60 for the mileage and 4 hours travel at $25, or another $160, and then surcharges $65 for the sea trial. This totals an additional $225, for a final bill of $725. If he does not survey the engine, you are obligated to accept the survey without the machinery portion, or hire an engine surveyor at $50 to $65 per hour, portal to portal. They generally take about five to six hours on the job. Now the bill has another $300 to $390 charge, for a theoretical $1,000-plus for an expense you had allowed $500 to cover.

Marine surveying is a business, and after 15 years of running one, I don't think surveyors can exist profitably without earning about $50 per hour, including travel time, time aboard the vessel, and time to prepare the survey in final form. The job is only half done at the completion of the fieldwork. The surveyor must then return to his office and work half the next day preparing the report. Using the same boat, let us say we travel 4 hours, survey aboard the vessel (4 hours, including engine), and prepare the report (another 2 hours). The totals are then 10 hours at $50 per hour, or $500, which corresponds to the flat $12.50 per foot. As boats get larger, the time aboard for survey increases, as does the time for preparing the report. As you can see, if the travel is extensive—more than 4 hours—and the boat large, I quote a rate of $15 per foot, and I'm not sure I break even on these. I do a lot of work on Long Island, which involves getting up at 5 A.M.; driving from Marblehead, Massachusetts, to New London, Connecticut; taking the ferry to Greenport,

New York; driving another hour; working the boat; doing the sea trials; back on the ferry; and back to Marblehead at 11 P.M. That's an 18-hour day. I've got to charge $850 to operate, and I am useless the next day! In other words, I cannot go to Long Island for a 30-foot survey and make any money. It has to be in the $15-a-foot category, which for my firm is over 50 feet.

If you get quotes from a surveyor to do these types of jobs at, say, $8 to $10 per foot, something is wrong! Either the surveyor is moonlighting or has no business overhead to support. The risk here is that you get an apprentice or unqualified surveyor whose work is totally unknown to the underwriters. They may refuse to accept the survey and ask for another prepared by someone they recognize. This happens when companies such as BOAT/U.S. request surveys. They have a recommended list of approved surveyors who understand exactly what they require in a survey report. If they do not get this type of report, back it comes to you, and you are out of pocket the first survey cost with no coverage.

These are the basic methods I am aware of by which surveyors compute their fees. Just ask about additional charges, and especially whether the machinery is included in the survey. If you are considering a company such as BOAT/U.S. or AVEMCO as your underwriter, be sure the surveyor you select is acceptable to them.

Chapter 8

Determining the Worth of Your Boat

If you own a production boat built in the last 30 years, the chances are good that the *BUC Used Boat Guide* will show a listing for it and an estimated high and low market value, based on the condition and model in question. This reference is published semiannually in three volumes by BUC Research, 1314 NE 17th Court, Ft. Lauderdale, FL 33305. In 1990, Volume 1 ($65) covered boats built in 1982 through 1988; Volume 2 ($55) covered 1972 through 1981, and Volume 3 ($45) covered 1905 through 1971. The guide takes into consideration the geographic location of the boat by adjusting the market values up or down. Such variations are mainly the result of supply and demand. Used boats in the northwest United States command a premium of 20 to 25 percent over the same boats marketed in the Northeast. The guide differentiates between gasoline-powered and diesel-equipped vessels, sloops, ketches and yawls, shoal- and deep-draft models. The BUC guide is widely used by banks and insurance companies to help determine the appropriate range of value for a given boat. Usually the surveyor's estimate of value will fall somewhere near these values, but not always. The guide's accuracy depends on actual reported sales of brokers and dealers throughout the U.S. Since the reporting is voluntary, many dealers do not keep it up to date, or they "fudge" the figures on the high side to keep resale prices high.

After four or five years, or if a boat goes out of production, some of the guide's prices may be way off the mark. The best source of what boats sell for is a yacht broker. I have a network of contacts in this business, and when I want to know what a boat is really worth, I talk with three or four of them. They will know of a recent sale or two from their own organization, or they will send me a printout from the BUC computerized listing network. This printout shows me every boat of the model in question offered for sale in the U.S., Canada, the Caribbean, and even in Europe. I can then adjust these offering prices by geographical location, assume from experience that the sale price will be 10 to 20 percent below the offering price, and come up with a very accurate real-world value.

In the last six years, the NADA publication, so well known for used cars, has also come out with a *Used Boat Price Guide*. I have found this publication more accurate in pricing smaller powerboats than sailing craft.

For many years, a used boat's value was pretty well defined by the price of a comparable new boat. But since 1989 the current Boat Depression has driven a great many manufacturers out of business, eliminating our basis for comparison. Also, by the late 1980s, prices of new boats had gotten so high that no one would buy them, because so many relatively new used boats were available at prices some 30 to 40 percent less. What all this means is that in normal periods of economic growth, prices are more predictable, but in distressed times, such as now, the guides are not nearly as reliable as using the computer and talking to the brokers about recent sales. Which is another way of saying it's a buyer's market out there.

The single biggest factor in retaining good resale value to my mind is the continued production of a particular model over a long period of time. A good example is the Hinckley Bermuda 40, first built about 1963 and in continuous production for more than 25 years. Other boats that come to mind are the Cape Dory 28 and 30; Pearson 35; Cal 40; C & C 27, 35, and 40; Sabre 28 and 34; J-30, 35, and 40; Catalina 30; Bristol 40, and later the 35.5 and 38.8.

Certain equipment adds to the desirability of a boat. Diesel engines are a major advantage and can add as much as $5,000 to the value of a given 40-foot model, the sistership of which has a gasoline auxiliary. Recently installed radar and GPS are a plus, but a big sail inventory (unless *brand*-new), VHF radios, Lorans, satnavs, and the like have little used value. A good-quality roller reefing headsail system, a Hood Stowaway or Reckmann mainsail system, or a new, fully battened main will increase market value. Fixed autopilots are a nice touch, although the everyday portable systems do not alter prices very much. Sophisticated instrumentation for racing, such as the Okam or a digital multifunction Brookes and Gatehouse nav system, also increase a boat's resale value.

What about cosmetics? This really counts a great deal. Buyers will always pay more for a cosmetically well-maintained boat—and I mean 10, 15, or 20 percent more than for a shabby-looking boat that still functions perfectly well in all respects. The value of cleanliness is not at all linear! If you had a $30,000 boat for sale, and you spent $500 to have it completely machine-cleaned and waxed, painted the dirty bilges, detailed the engine paint, and made it spotless, you could probably sell it for $2,000 more. That is a very good return on your investment.

New machinery in older boats enhances the price over and above what your BUC and broker research tell you, because the guides assume original equipment in good working order. A new, low-hour engine or generator increases value nearly dollar for dollar in the first year of use.

Condition

What detracts most from the market value of your boat? The three major areas are structural problems, cosmetic damage or neglect, and badly worn or inoperative machinery.

Structural Problems

Among structural problems, a wet hull, deck, or both caused by previous damage or osmosis rank high. I see more deck problems than hull problems because most decks are cored, and there are more fittings on deck than on the hull. When you have a clear-cut saturation of one or both, the market values as determined by the various methods I have discussed are invalid. Often the boat becomes a total constructive loss, by which I mean that the cost to repair it exceeds more than, say, 70 percent of the estimated market value. For example:

> Pearson 30, 1977; market value 1992, $14,000.
> Damage: Saturated hull laminates, wet deck core.
> Cost of hull repairs (full peel of hull; prep, dry, and relaminate; seal bottom with Interprotect 3000 system): $9,000.
> Repair of deck core (remove old core, install new, resurface deck as necessary): $10,000.
> Total repairs: $19,000.

In this case, the repairs exceed the market value, which means the seller/owner of the boat has to accept almost anything for it, or simply dispose of it, because it cannot pass a marine survey. The cost for disposing of a 30-foot fiberglass boat runs about $200 a foot, but usually you can sell the engine, rigging, sails, electronics, lead ballast, and other equipment. If you find yourself in this position, you may be better off selling the boat for next to nothing. This at least saves the yard bills and the cost of destroying the hull. This is only a theoretical case, but there are plenty of real ones out there!

Failed Machinery or Rigging

A dead engine or a broken mast reduces the total value of the boat by much more than the cost of repowering or rerigging. I think this should be called the inconvenience penalty, because many people look at problems like these and think first about the time and aggravation involved in any large repair, which is true! A Pearson 30 with a blown Atomic Four gas engine, for instance, might bring offers of $4,000 to $5,000, or even less. The cost of a Yanmar 2GMF diesel and gear (installed) for this boat is about $7,500, and the new diesel improves the normal market value, which assumes a gas engine in good working order. So instead of taking a real licking, the owner can commission the repair and get maybe $18,000 to $20,000 for his boat. Conversely, of course, a buyer may be able to find a great buy this way, in exchange for a little aggravation.

The cost of a mast and standing rigging for this boat might be $5,000, and makes it more marketable, but the potential for an increase in value is less than what can be realized by installing a new engine or generator.

Cosmetics

Good looks, as I have said, are worth a lot to a buyer and a seller. It establishes the all-important first impression and tells the buyer that the owner took good care of his boat in other ways, too. If you are dealing with a badly faded hull color, or topsides that have been severely gouged in numerous areas, you can expect to receive 10 to 25 percent less than the indicated market value, which assumes "average" good condition. The most striking improvement one can make to a vessel in poor condition is to repaint it with Imron, Awlgrip, Sterling, or Interspray 800—high-quality two-part polyurethane paints. The cost of this improvement is about $125 per foot (prices vary from region to region), including prep work, priming, and painting. In order to recoup the money spent on the painting, the boat will have to be more valuable than the Pearson 30 I used as an example. The cost to repaint this boat is $3,750, which would be hard to pass along 100 percent. However, if you have a 40-foot boat that potentially will sell for $60,000 but is worth only $48,000 because it looks bad, a $5,000 paint job would be well justified.

Repainting and repowering give you the best return on your investment. Simple cosmetics, such as maintaining brightwork, keeping interior cushions like new, cleaning and painting bilges and lockers, adding or maintaining dodgers and other canvas, replacing clouded Plexiglas ports with Lexan, and keeping a well-detailed engine room will add immeasurably to the value of your boat.

Appendix

Compliance Items

In addition to ascertaining the condition of the hull, deck, machinery, and rigging, surveyors are required by federal and state regulations to inspect specific equipment on pleasure craft. The three agencies that govern which equipment must be inspected are the Coast Guard, through CFR 33 and 46 regulations; the National Fire Protection Agency, through its code 302; and lastly, the American Boat and Yacht Council Inc., a private organization that works with boat manufacturers to publish a large volume on acceptable boatbuilding practices.

Coast Guard (Federal Regulations)

Some of these items are required by federal laws—such as the Coast Guard regulations that cover, among other things, display of registration numbers. Surveyors must check these items. Most of the federal laws stipulate what safety equipment must be on board, which differs for commercial vessels and pleasure boats. Personal flotation devices (Type I, II, III, IV, and V) and firefighting equipment (including approved fixed systems such as CO_2 or Halon, and portable B-1 and B-2 dry chemical extinguishers), for example, are among the common safety-related compliance items for pleasure boats.

Flares, horns, and life rings fall under this category of inspection, and it is the surveyor's responsibility to note all discrepancies.

One of the better-known federal requirements is the holding-tank requirement. All vessels equipped with a nonportable head must have a type I, II, or II marine sanitation device for retention and or treatment of waste.

Federal law further requires that a sign prohibiting the discharge of oil be displayed in or close to machinery spaces. A similar warning sign detailing the operation of LPG and CNG stoves or heating devices must be displayed in the proximity of the unit.

In the engine and fuel-storage compartments, vessels built before 1980 require two ventilators; vessels built after 1980 require a "motorized ventilation system," commonly referred to as a blower.

Flame (backfire) arrestors, to be fitted over carburetors in gas engines, and the type of Coast Guard–approved fuel lines that are acceptable (Type A or Type B) are also specified.

Included in the federal list of compliance items are navigational lights. The specific requirements differ depending on, among other things, the length of the vessel and whether it is a power- or sailboat.

You can obtain a copy of the Department of Transportation's publication on federal requirements for recreational boaters from the U.S. Government Printing Office, Superintendent of Documents, Washington, DC 20402.

The National Fire Protection Agency (NFPA)

The NFPA publishes the fire-protection standards for pleasure and commercial craft under its NFPA 302 edition. This agency, started in 1925, covers the full range of fire-protection standards used in the United States. The text is some 45 pages long. The more important aspects to the surveyor and boatowner are highlighted below.

Where the Coast Guard list may state "blower required," the NFPA enumerates (i.e., the engine blower in question shall have a rating for continuous operation at 120 percent of nominal voltage, shall meet Underwriters Laboratory [UL] specifications, etc.). They also describe where blowers can be installed. The NFPA codes are used by all marine underwriters in assessing risks, and failure to comply with these codes is in itself reason enough to fail a survey. Like the federal regulations, the NFPA standards are must-comply items.

Other salient points covered by the NFPA 302 are:

- General principles of lightning protection
- hull ventilation, natural and forced
- marine carburetors
- engine exhaust systems
- hose connections in engine rooms
- materials used in engine rooms
- fuel systems
- fuel lines
- fuel tanks and materials
- fuel tank grounds
- design and construction of fuel tanks
- tank installations
- fill and vents for fuel tanks
- installation of LPG and CNG appliance systems
- storage and ventilation of LPG systems
- reducing regulators for LPG and CNG systems
- pressure gauges on gas systems
- cabin heaters and hotwater heaters (gas)
- ignition protection systems
- circuit breakers
- main electrical panels
- polarity systems
- voltage rating for wiring
- battery installation
- terminal connections
- GFCI breakers
- 115 AC wiring requirements

The NFPA 302 codes are available from the NFPA, 1 Batterymarch Park, P.O. Box 9101, Quincy, MA 02269-9101.

American Boat and Yacht Council (ABYC)

This organization was founded in 1954 with the express purpose of joining the public, the boating industry, and the government to develop boating standards and recommended practices that would result in better-quality, safer boats. Membership is open to the public, and a current copy of the

Standards and Recommended Practices for Small Craft, is available from the ABYC, 3069 Solomon's Island Road, Edgewater, MD 21037; 410-974-8712.

This publication is likely to be used more by boatbuilders and designers than owners (the member price is $75.00, nonmembers pay $150.00). Much of the material overlaps the NFPA codes. It is divided into machinery, electrical, equipment, and engineering sections, and has recommendations on everything from buoyancy, cathodic protection, and compass installations to seacock installation and the correct numbering of hulls. If you were planning to retrofit an older boat, a copy of this publication and the NFPA 302, would cover all the code and installation areas you would need to do the job properly.

A condensed version, *Rules and Regulations for Recreational Boaters* is also available from The ABYC ($17.50 for members, $22.50 for nonmembers).

These standards comprise all that is presently thought to be in the best interest of boating safety. You will be much better off owning a vessel that complies with them, and it is a great advantage to the boat shopper to be able to recognize good or bad practices. Federal and state laws have become much more stringent regarding individual compliance, and fines are commonplace.

Index

Note: Numbers in **boldface type** refer to illustrations.